Contents

About the Author

Patrice-Anne Rutledge is a business technology author and journalist specializing in social media, online applications, and small business technology. Her other books include *Sams Teach Yourself LinkedIn in 10 Minutes*, *Using LinkedIn*, *Using Facebook*, and *The Truth About Profiting from Social Networking*, all from Pearson. Through Rutledge Communications, she also offers writing and editing services to businesses and nonprofits worldwide. You can reach Patrice through her website at www.patricerutledge.com.

Dedication

To my family, with thanks for their ongoing support and encouragement.

Acknowledgments

Special thanks to Rick Kughen, Karen Weinstein, Betsy Harris, and Sam Sinkhorn for their feedback, suggestions, and attention to detail.

We Want to Hear from You!

As the reader of this book, *you* are our most important critic and commentator. We value your opinion and want to know what we're doing right, what we could do better, what areas you'd like to see us publish in, and any other words of wisdom you're willing to pass our way.

You can email or write me directly to let me know what you did or didn't like about this book—as well as what we can do to make our books stronger.

Please note that I cannot help you with technical problems related to the topic of this book, and that due to the high volume of mail I receive, I might not be able to reply to every message.

When you write, please be sure to include this book's title and author as well as your name and phone or email address. I will carefully review your comments and share them with the author and editors who worked on the book.

E-mail: consumer@samspublishing.com

Mail: Greg Wiegand
Editor-in-Chief
Sams Publishing
800 East 96th Street
Indianapolis, IN 46240 USA

Reader Services

Visit our website and register this book at informit.com/register for convenient access to any updates, downloads, or errata that might be available for this book.

Introduction

Google+ is Google's answer to social sharing on the web. Soon after its launch of a limited field trial on June 28, 2011, Google+ already had tens of millions of members with thousands more joining every day, eagerly seeking out invitations from friends and colleagues. When Google+ opened to the public in mid-September 2011, its user base jumped more than 30 percent within days.

If you use other social sites such as Facebook, LinkedIn, or Twitter, the basic concepts of Google+ should seem familiar to you. You can post text-based updates, photos, videos, and links; comment on posts from people you know and follow; share interesting content from around the web; and much more. Google+ has several unique features as well, such as the power to maintain complete control over how you share each piece of content you post. Google+ also extends beyond traditional social networking to offer unlimited uploading and storage of photos and videos, video chats, group text messaging, and more.

Sams Teach Yourself Google+ in 10 Minutes is designed to get you up and running on Google+ as quickly as possible. This book is based on the Google+ beta. Because Google+ is still under development and its functionality will continue to change over time, the features available to you may vary at any given time. The companion website to this book will help keep you updated on what's new with Google+. For now, turn to Lesson 1, "Introducing Google+," to get started with this powerful social-sharing tool.

Who Is This Book For?

This book is for you if...

- ► You're new to Google+ and want to learn what it's all about.

- ► You want to share content, photos, and videos on the web with friends, family, and colleagues and heard that Google+ is a great way to do this.

▶ You want to become productive on Google+ as quickly as possible and are short on time.

Companion Website

This book has a companion website online at http://www.patricerutledge. com/books/google-plus.

Visit the site to access the following:

▶ Book updates

▶ News about Google+ enhancements and features

▶ Other books and articles that may be of interest to you

Conventions Used in This Book

The Teach Yourself series has several unique elements that will help you as you are learning more about Google+. These include the following:

> NOTE: A note presents interesting pieces of information related to the surrounding discussion.

> TIP: A tip offers advice or teaches an easier way to do something.

> CAUTION: A caution advises you about potential problems and helps you steer clear of disaster.

> PLAIN ENGLISH: Plain English icons provide clear definitions of new, essential terms.

LESSON 1
Introducing Google+

In this lesson, you explore Google+ and learn how to set up your Google+ account.

Exploring Google+

Google+ is Google's social networking site that emphasizes real-life sharing where you're in control of exactly who sees—or doesn't see—your content. Launched on June 28, 2011, Google+ has tens of millions of users, with thousands of new users joining every day.

In addition to its extensive social sharing features, Google+ also enables you to chat with friends via text and video, upload unlimited photos and videos, play games, and more. Google+ integrates automatically with other Google applications you may already use including Buzz, Profiles, Picasa, Gmail, and more.

Currently, you can create a Google+ profile only for an individual person. Google+ profiles for business are tentatively scheduled for release in late 2011. If you want to use Google+ for business before this release, you can create profiles for individual people in your company and then create a company profile when this feature is available.

If you use other social sites such as Facebook, LinkedIn, or Twitter, the basic concepts of Google+ should be familiar to you. Google+ has several unique features, however, and its own terminology. You'll learn more about each of these features as you read through this book, but for now, it's a good idea to become familiar with these Google+ terms:

> ▶ **Profile.** Your profile is your public presence on Google+ that includes your photo, information about your background, and links to your other sites on the web. If you use Facebook or

LinkedIn, the concept of a profile should be familiar to you. With Google+, you have control over each section on your profile and can specify exactly who can see that section. For example, you can display a detailed profile to people you know and reveal less information to those you don't. To view a sample Google+ profile, visit my profile at https://plus.google.com/108294135476012165013.

NOTE: How Can I Shorten My Google+ Profile URL?

By default, your Google+ profile URL includes a 21-digit identifier. Google+ doesn't offer custom URLs at this time, but you can use a third-party tool such as gplus.to (http://gplus.to) or Plusya (http://plusya.com) to create a custom URL. For example, my Google+ profile shortened with gplus.to is http://gplus.to/PatriceRutledge.

▶ **Circles.** Circles enable you to organize your Google+ network by placing people into distinct groups, such as Family, Friends, and Acquaintances. When you post content on Google+, you can specify exactly which circles can view each post. You can also specify privacy settings by circle. This gives you complete control over who sees what content. Placing people in a Google+ circle is similar to following people on Twitter. They don't need to accept a formal request and can choose whether they want to place you in one of their circles (in other words, whether they want to follow you back).

▶ **Stream.** The Google+ stream offers a central location for viewing the posts, links, photos, and videos that you and others have shared. You can join the conversation on the stream by adding your own posts and comments, sharing interesting content you discover, and supporting quality posts using the Google +1 button. If you're familiar with Facebook, the Google+ stream is similar to the Facebook wall but with added privacy controls.

▶ **+1 button.** The Google +1 button offers a way to publicly show your support for a post that you like. The +1 button is available on Google+ and, optionally, on other websites and blogs that choose to enable this button. Google+ uses the term "+1" as both a noun and verb. Using Google+ terminology, you +1 a post using the +1 button. In many ways, the +1 button is similar to the Like button on Facebook.

▶ **Google+ bar.** The Google+ bar is a handy toolbar that displays at the top of any Google product, including Google+, Google (the search engine), Gmail, Google Reader, and so forth. This bar offers easy access to the most popular Google+ features. You must be signed in to your Google+ account to have full access to the Google+ bar.

▶ **Hangouts.** Hangouts enable you to get together with other Google+ users using live video chat. You can even watch a YouTube video together during a hangout.

▶ **Huddle.** Participate in group texting, either one-on-one or with the people in one of your Google+ circles. You can invite others to a huddle or receive a notification on your status bar when someone invites you to a huddle. This feature is currently available only for the Google+ Android app and Google+ iPhone app.

▶ **Instant Upload.** Upload photos and videos automatically from your Android 2.1+ smartphone to a private Google+ album. You can later make any photos or videos public if you choose to share them.

Signing Up for Google+

Google+ requires you to have an existing Google account. If you already use another Google product—such as Gmail, AdWords, Buzz, or Reader— you have a Google account. For example, you can use your Gmail address to sign up for Google+. If you don't have a Google account, you can sign up for one when you sign up for Google+. In addition, you must be at least 18 years old to participate on Google+.

To sign up for Google+, follow these steps:

1. Navigate to https://plus.google.com, as shown in Figure 1.1.

FIGURE 1.1   Signing up for Google+ takes just a few minutes.

2. If you aren't signed in to your Google account, click the **Sign In** button to open Google's sign-in page and enter your email and password. If you are signed in to your Google account, you don't need to sign in again.

NOTE: **How Do I Sign Up for a Google Account?**

If you don't have an existing Google account, click the **Create an Account** link on the Google+ page. The **Create an Account** page opens, where you can sign up for a Google account. When you're done, return to the Google+ page to sign up for Google+.

---

3. Verify that your first and last names are correct on the Google+ sign-up page, shown in Figure 1.2. By default, Google+ uses the first and last name fields from your email account.

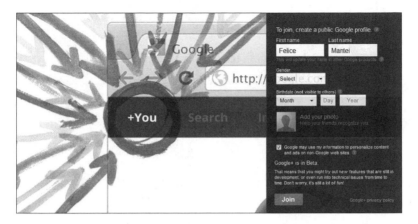

FIGURE 1.2   Google+ connects with your existing Google account.

TIP: **You Can Also Sign Up for Google+ By Responding to an Invitation**

If a friend invites you to Google+, you'll receive your invitation by email. Click the **Join Google+** button in the email you receive. If your email address is associated with a Google account, the Google+ sign-up page displays (refer to Figure 1.2). If Google doesn't recognize your email address, you're prompted to sign in to your Google account or create a new account.

CAUTION: **You Must Use Your Real Name on Google+**

Google+ requires that you use your real name when creating a Google+ profile. You can't create your own username or use a pseudonym. If you have privacy concerns, you can specify exactly who has access to the information you post on Google+.

---

4. Select your **Gender** from the drop-down list.

5. Enter your **Birthdate**. Google+ uses this to determine age-appropriate content to display. This date isn't visible to other Google+ users.

6. Click the **Add Your Photo** link to open the **Select Profile Photo** dialog box, shown in Figure 1.3.

7. Click the **Select a Photo from Your Computer** button.

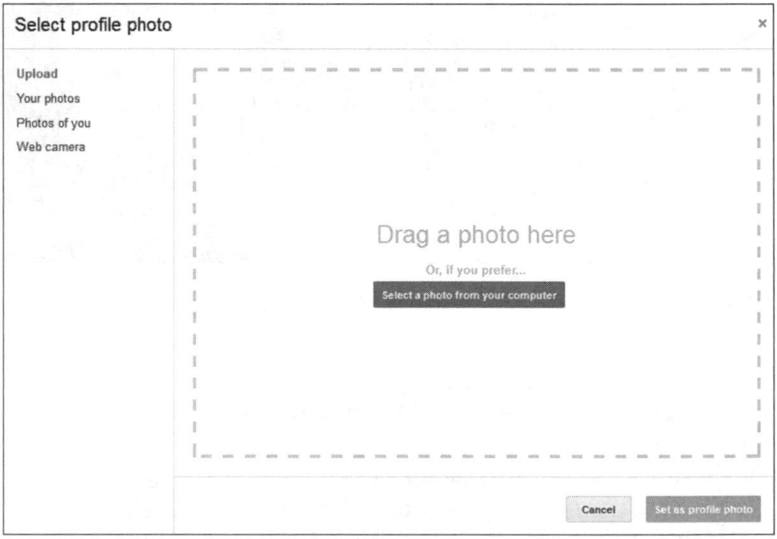

| Select profile photo | × |

Upload
Your photos
Photos of you
Web camera

Drag a photo here

Or, if you prefer...

Select a photo from your computer

Cancel   Set as profile photo

FIGURE 1.3   Select a photo to display on your Google+ profile.

TIP: **Add a Photo Using Drag and Drop**

Optionally, you can drag and drop a photo to the **Select Profile Photo** dialog box. For example, if you have Windows Explorer open in a separate, minimized window, you can select your photo and drag it to this dialog box.

8. In the **File Upload** dialog box, select the photo you want to upload and click the **Open** button. Depending on your browser and operating system, this dialog box and button could have different names.

9. In the **Select Profile Photo** dialog box, shown in Figure 1.4, drag the four white squares that surround your photo to crop it to the desired size.

FIGURE 1.4 Crop your photo to fit in the space provided.

TIP: Quickly Fix Problems with Your Photo

Optionally, you can click the **Rotate Left** or **Rotate Right** icons next to your photo to fix rotation problems. If you need to fix cosmetic issues such as red eye or color contrast, click the **Picnik** link to open Picnik (www.picnik.com), a web-based photo-editing application where you can enhance your photo.

---

10. Click the **Set as Profile Photo** button. Google+ returns to the sign-up box where your photo now displays (see Figure 1.5).

11. By default, Google uses your information to personalize content and ads on non-Google websites. If you don't want Google to use your Google+ data to personalize ads in this manner, remove the checkmark from the checkbox that displays below your photo.

12. Click the **Join** button to join Google+.

To join, create a public Google profile.

First name
Felice

Last name
Mantei

This will update your name in other Google products.

Gender
Female

Birthdate (not visible to others)
January   12   1972

Change photo
Help your friends recognize you.

☑ Google may use my information to personalize content
and ads on non-Google web sites.

Google+ is in Beta.

That means that you might try out new features that are still in
development, or even run into technical issues from time to
time. Don't worry, it's still a lot of fun!

Join   Google+ privacy policy

FIGURE 1.5   Return to the sign-up page to finish the sign-up process.

13. Google+ prompts you to enter basic profile data, such as the
    school you attended, your employer, and the places you lived
    (see Figure 1.6). When you start typing the name of a school or
    employer, Google+ displays a drop-down list of potential
    matches for you to choose from. Although entering this data is
    optional, it makes it easier for the people you know to find you.

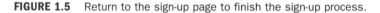

Add additional profile information to your public profile.
Adding more information will help your friends, family, and others find and connect with you.

School	School name	Year
Where you work	Employer	Job title
Where you live	Enter a city or a country	

FIGURE 1.6   Add details about your schools, employers, and places you've
lived.

> NOTE: **You Can Expand Your Profile After Signing Up for Google+**
>
> Google+ asks you to enter basic profile data during the sign-up process, but you can expand your profile later, even specifying exactly who can see each section of your profile. See Lesson 2, "Working with Google+ Profiles," for more information.

14. Click the **Change Profile Photo** button if you want to change the profile photo you uploaded. If you're satisfied with your profile photo, you can skip this step.

15. Click the **Continue** button in the lower-left corner of the screen.

16. Optionally, you can search for your email contacts on sites such as Yahoo! or Hotmail. In general, however, it's a good idea to complete your profile first before connecting with others. Click the **Skip** button to skip this step for now.

17. Google+ prompts you to add people to circles, suggesting several people you might know (see Figure 1.7). Your options usually include the person who invited you as well as people in this person's circles. You can add people to circles now or add them later. In general, it's a good idea to understand how circles work and affect your privacy before adding a lot of people to circles. See Lesson 3, "Managing Your Network with Circles," for more information. Click the **Continue** button to go to the next step.

18. Google+ prompts you to add some well-know people and celebrities to your circles, as shown in Figure 1.8. Again, you can do this now or wait until you've learned more about circles. If you want to add people now, it's recommended to add celebrities to your **Following** circle because you don't actually know them. Click the **Continue** button to go to the next step.

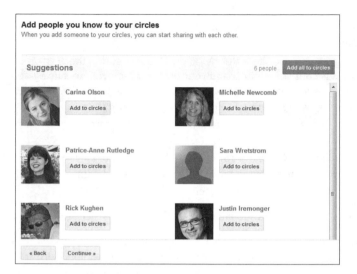

FIGURE 1.7   See if you recognize any familiar faces to add to your circles.

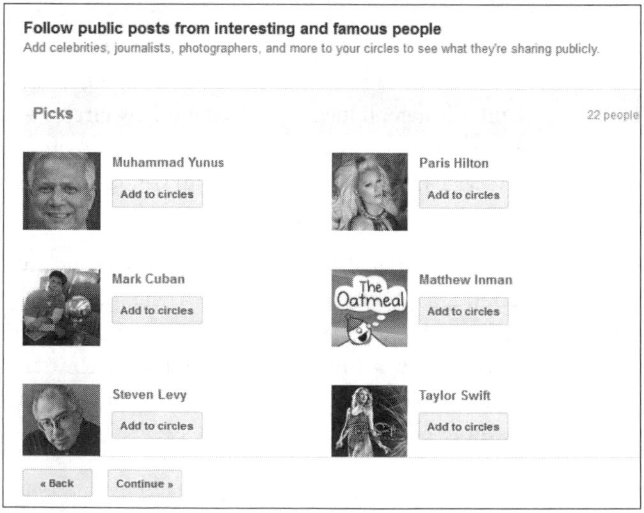

FIGURE 1.8   You can also follow posts by your favorite celebrities.

Google+ opens, displaying your stream (see Figure 1.9).

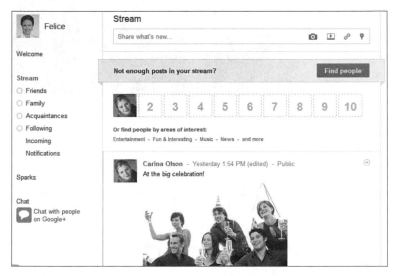

FIGURE 1.9   Your stream displays posts from people in your circles.

Your stream displays the posts of the people you added to circles during steps 17 and 18. If you haven't added anyone yet, your stream is empty—for now.

From here, you can complete your profile, add people to circles, specify your privacy settings, and then start participating on Google+ by adding your own content and commentary. You can also visit the Google+ Welcome page by clicking the Welcome link on the left side of the page. The Welcome page includes videos about the most innovative features on Google+ and also gives you suggestions on things to do to make the most of your Google+ experience.

Signing In to Google+

After you have a Google+ account, you can sign in by going to the Google+ website (https://plus.google.com), clicking the **Sign In** button, and entering your email address and password (see Figure 1.10).

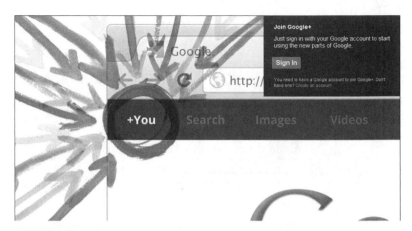

FIGURE 1.10   Sign in to Google+ by entering your Google account email and password.

If you're already signed in to another Google application (such as Gmail), click your first name in the upper-left corner of the Google+ bar to open Google+ (see Figure 1.11). Be aware that you must have signed up for Google+ for this link to be available.

FIGURE 1.11   You can also access Google+ from the Google+ bar.

Summary

In this first lesson, you learned about the many features Google+ offers and how to sign up for an account. Next, it's time to create a more detailed profile.

LESSON 2

Working with Google+ Profiles

In this lesson, you learn how to edit and manage your Google+ profile.

Understanding Google+ Profiles

When you first sign up for Google+, your profile contains only basic information. Figure 2.1 shows a sample profile for a new Google+ user.

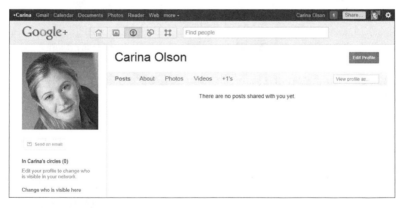

FIGURE 2.1 Your profile is a blank canvas when you first sign up for Google+.

Figure 2.2 shows a sample completed Google+ profile.

FIGURE 2.2   A complete profile lets people know who you are and generates better results.

NOTE: **Why Does My Profile Already Contain Content?**
If you created a profile using Google Profiles (https://profiles.google.com) before the launch of Google+, Google uses this content as the basis for your initial Google+ profile.

Although you can customize your profile content, all Google+ profiles follow the same basic layout:

▶ The Google+ bar displays across the top of your profile.

▶ Google+ navigation icons display directly below the Google+ bar.

▶ The left column displays your photo, the **Send an Email** button, and photos of people from your circles.

▶ The right column displays your name, headline, profile tabs with custom content, and an optional series of up to five photos.

Before sharing content on Google+ and adding people to circles, you should enhance your profile with more detailed content and specify your preferred profile privacy settings.

As you add more content to your profile, consider carefully how you plan to use Google+. Do you want to communicate primarily with family and friends? Are you sharing content with professional colleagues? Or are you using your personal profile to promote your business? Thinking about your goals and target audience can help you determine what to post on your profile and which privacy settings to select.

CAUTION: **Don't Use a Personal Profile to Create a Business Presence**
Google+ profiles are designed for individual people using their own name, not for businesses, brands, or other organizations. Google plans to introduce Google+ profiles for business later in 2011.

Editing Your Google+ Profile

Google+ enables you to edit your profile, choosing the exact content to display on it and specifying who can view it.

In addition to editing the content on your Google+ profile, you can change your profile photo or display a series of photos at the top of your profile. See Lesson 8, "Working with Photos," for more information about using photos on Google+.

Editing Your Profile's About Tab

To edit your profile's **About** tab, follow these steps:

1. Click the **Profile** icon at the top of Google+, as shown in Figure 2.3.

Click to edit your profile.

FIGURE 2.3   Click the Profile icon to edit your profile.

2. Click the **Edit Profile** button in the upper-right corner of the page.

3. On the **About** tab, which opens by default, click the section you want to edit and enter your content. Only sections for which you add content display on your profile. Figure 2.4 shows the sections available for edit on the **About** tab.

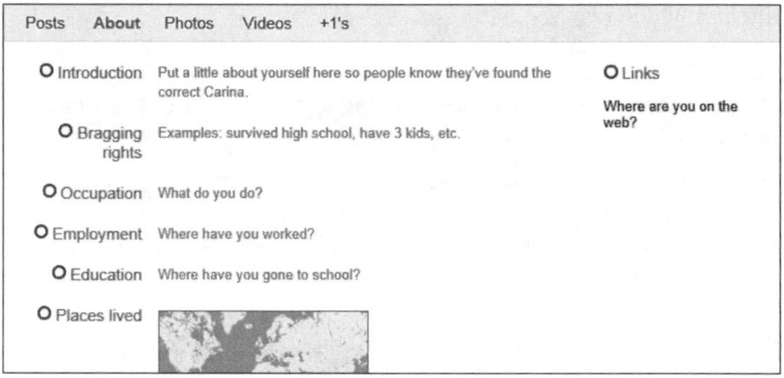

| Posts | **About** | Photos | Videos | +1's |

○ Introduction   Put a little about yourself here so people know they've found the correct Carina.

○ Bragging rights   Examples: survived high school, have 3 kids, etc.

○ Occupation   What do you do?

○ Employment   Where have you worked?

○ Education   Where have you gone to school?

○ Places lived

○ Links

Where are you on the web?

FIGURE 2.4   Choose the sections you want to display on your About tab.

These sections include:

▶ **Introduction.** Add a paragraph or two about yourself. The Introduction dialog box includes buttons that enable you to bold, italicize, and underline text; add bulleted and numbered lists; and add links to external websites. If you make a mistake, click the **Remove Formatting** button to remove any formatting you applied. Figure 2.5 shows the Introduction dialog box.

▶ **Bragging Rights.** Let people know about accomplishments you're proud of—both personal and professional.

▶ **Occupation.** Enter your occupation or professional headline in the text box.

▶ **Employment.** Start typing your company name and Google+ displays potential matches from existing profiles. For example, if you work for Pearson Education, a drop-down list displays this company when you start to type its name (see Figure 2.6). Optionally, enter your title and

employment dates for each job and click the **Current**
checkbox if you're currently employed with that company.
If you make a mistake, click the **Remove Item** button (**X**)
to delete a row.

FIGURE 2.5   You can format text and add links to your introduction.

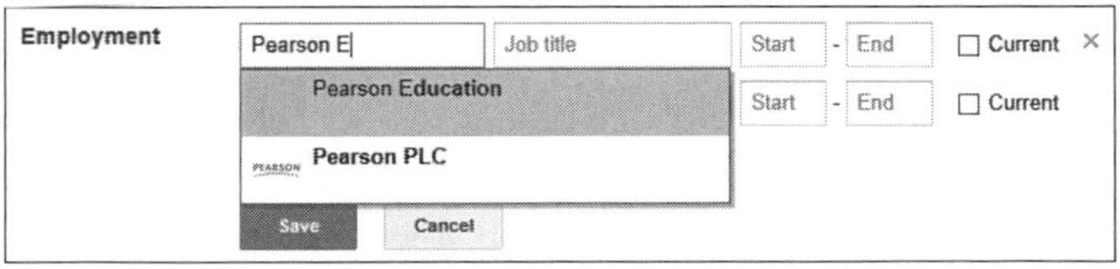

FIGURE 2.6   Google+ displays potential employer matches in a drop-down
list.

► **Education.** Start typing your school name and Google+
displays potential matches from existing profiles. For
example, if you attended Stanford University, a drop-down
list displays this school when you start to type its name.
Optionally, enter your major and attendance dates for each
school and click the **Current** checkbox if you're a current
student. If you make a mistake, click the **Remove Item**
button (**X**) to delete a row.

▶ **Places Lived.** Type the names of cities where you've lived to display them on a map on your profile.

▶ **Home.** Enter your home contact information, such as your home phone number, mobile phone number, email address, and so forth. If you choose to enter data in this section, be sure to consider your privacy options carefully.

▶ **Work.** Enter your work contact information, such as your work phone number, mobile phone number, email address, and so forth. If you choose to enter data in this section, be sure to consider your privacy options carefully.

▶ **Relationship.** Select one of ten relationship status options if you want to broadcast your personal status to your Google+ friends.

▶ **Looking For.** Select one of the following relationship goals if you want to let others know what you're looking for: friends, dating, a relationship, or networking.

▶ **Gender.** Select one of the three options Google+ provides: male, female, or other.

▶ **Other Names.** Enter other names, such as a maiden name.

▶ **Nickname.** Enter a nickname if you use one. For example, your profile could list you as Robert William Covington III, but your friends could call you Bill.

▶ **Search Visibility.** Specify whether you want to make your profile available in search results, such as on Google, Yahoo!, or Bing. This option is most useful if you want to use your profile to promote a business or your expertise as a job candidate.

4. Select your privacy options for each section from the drop-down list. See "Specifying Profile Privacy by Section" next in this lesson for more information.

5. Click the **Save** button to save your changes for each section.

6. Click the **Done Editing** button at the top of the Google+ page.

Specifying Profile Privacy by Section

To specify who can view a profile section, click the drop-down list on that section to display the privacy options available (see Figure 2.7).

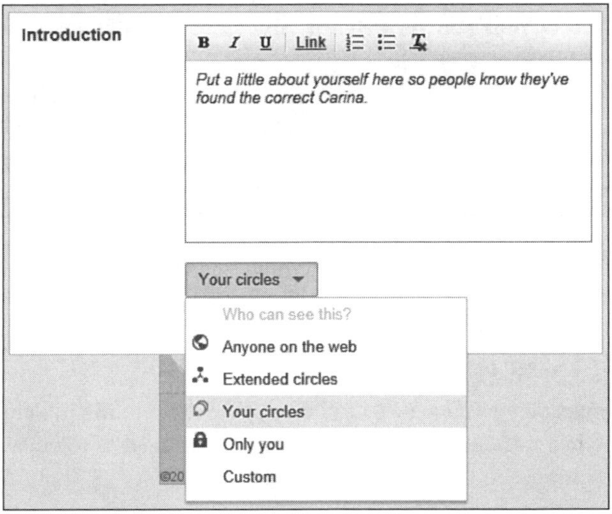

FIGURE 2.7   You have control over who sees each section of your profile.

Your options include:

- ▶ **Anyone on the Web.** Make the section public, available to anyone whether or not they are in your circles. This option is most suited to public figures or those who want to use their profile for marketing purposes.

- ▶ **Extended Circles.** Share with the people who are in your circles' circle. For example, if your friend Sara is in one of your circles, the people in her circles would also be able to view your content.

- ▶ **Your Circles.** Share with people in your own circles. This is the default selection.

- ▶ **Only You.** Ensure maximum privacy for this data. You're the only person who can view it. You can also simply delete the content in a section to remove it from your profile.

▶ **Custom.** Specify exactly who can view this section. For example, you could display a section to your "Family" and "Friends" circles, but not to your "Business" circle.

TIP: **Review Your Profile Privacy Any Time You Create New Circles**

If you want to restrict access to profile sections by circle, edit your profile again after creating new circles. See Lesson 3, "Managing Your Network with Circles," for more information about creating circles.

See Lesson 4, "Managing Google+ Settings and Privacy," for information about additional Google+ privacy options.

Adding Links on Your Google+ Profile

Adding links on your Google+ profile can help drive traffic to your other sites. You can add links to your website or blog as well as to other social sites such as Facebook, LinkedIn, or Twitter.

To add links on your Google+ profile, follow these steps:

1. Click the **Links** section on your profile to open the Links dialog box, shown in Figure 2.8.

FIGURE 2.8   Link to your website, blog, or other social site.

2. Click the **Add Custom Link** link.

> **TIP: Let Google+ Find Potential Links for You**
>
> If you already have accounts on other sites, Google+ finds them through your email address and displays them on the Links dialog box (see Figure 2.9). Google+ searches for Facebook, Yahoo!, Flickr, LinkedIn, Quora, Twitter, Yelp, Microsoft, MySpace, and Plaxo accounts. Click the **Add to Profile** button (a plus sign) to the right of any account to add it as a link on your Google+ profile.

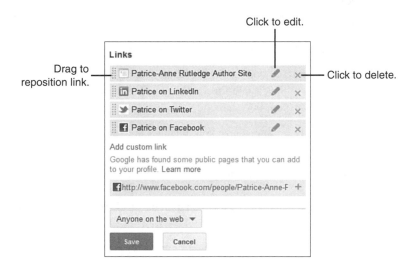

FIGURE 2.9   Google+ finds your other sites for you.

3. Enter the name for your link in the first text box. For example, if you want to link to your website or blog, enter its name.

4. Enter the complete URL of your website, such as http://www.patricerutledge.com.

5. Select the **This Page is Specifically About Me** checkbox if this link leads to your own personal content. For example, you should select this checkbox for your own website or blog but not for the website of a large corporation you work for.

> NOTE: **Why Does Google+ Want to Know if a Page Is About Me?**
> When you select this checkbox, Google+ displays content from the specified site on the +1's tab on your profile if you confirm authorship. An easy way to confirm authorship is to add the Google+ profile button to your site. See the "Adding a Google+ Profile Button to Your Website" section later in this lesson for more information. To learn more about the technical details of site authorship, click the **Learn More** link to the right of the **This Page is Specifically About Me** checkbox.

---

6. Repeat steps 3 through 5 until you finish adding links.

7. Select your privacy options for the Links section from the drop-down list. See "Specifying Profile Privacy by Section" earlier in this lesson for more information.

8. Click the **Save** button to save your changes and close the dialog box.

9. Click the **Done Editing** button at the top of the Google+ page.

Figure 2.10 shows an example of links on a Google+ profile.

FIGURE 2.10   Some sample links on a Google+ profile.

After adding links to your Google+ profile, you can:

▶ Change a link's display order by dragging the handle to the left of its name on the Link dialog box (refer to Figure 2.9).

▶ Edit the link content by clicking the **Edit Link** button.

▶ Delete the link by clicking the **Remove Item** button.

▶ Manage the accounts that Google+ found on its own by clicking the link. The **Connected Accounts** dialog box opens, where you can specify which accounts to display on your profile, remove an account, or connect an additional account.

Specifying the Tabs to Display on Your Profile

In addition to the **About** tab, Google+ profiles display several other tabs. You can choose which tabs to display and who can view them.

To specify which tabs to display on your profile, follow these steps:

1. Click the **Profile** icon at the top of the Google+ screen (refer to Figure 2.3).

2. Click the **Edit Profile** button in the upper-right corner of the page.

3. Select the tab you want to edit and make any changes. These include:

> ▶ **Posts.** Google+ requires you to display the **Posts** tab, so there are no edit options for posts. When people click this tab, they view your Google+ posts based on the security settings you applied to them.

> ▶ **Photos.** The **Photos** tab displays photos you uploaded to Google+. If you don't want to display this tab, remove the checkmark next to the **Show This Tab on Your Profile** checkbox and click the **Save** button (see Figure 2.11). See Lesson 8 for more information about the fields in this section and posting photos on Google+.

FIGURE 2.11   Control how photos display on your profile.

▶ **Videos.** The **Videos** tab displays videos you uploaded to Google+. If you don't want to display this tab, remove the checkmark next to the **Show This Tab on Your Profile** checkbox and click the **Save** button. See Lesson 5, "Sharing Content on Google+," for more information about posting videos on Google+.

▶ **+1's.** The **+1's** tab displays content from websites you identified as your own in the **Links** section of your profile. It also displays your +1 activity on other websites. For example, if you read an interesting blog post on another website and clicked the post's +1 button to show your support, it would display on this tab. If you don't want to display the +1's tab, remove the checkmark next to the **Show This Tab on Your Profile** checkbox and click the **Save** button.

▶ **Buzz.** The **Buzz** tab displays the Google Buzz content (www.google.com/buzz) associated with the email you use for Google+. If you don't want to display the **Buzz** tab, remove the checkmark next to the **Show This Tab on Your Profile** checkbox and click the **Save** button. Optionally, you can show a list of the people you're following and those who are following you as well as posts you've commented on or liked. If you don't use Google Buzz, this tab isn't available.

4. Click the **Done Editing** button at the top of the Google+ page.

Specifying Who Can Send You an Email

Optionally, you can allow your Google+ profile visitors to send you an email by displaying the Send an Email button on your profile. Using this button hides your actual email address from the people who contact you.

To specify who can view this button on your profile, follow these steps:

1. Click the **Profile** icon at the top of your Google+ page (refer to Figure 2.3).

2. Click the **Edit Profile** button in the upper-right corner of the page.

3. Click the **Send an Email** button below your photo.

4. If you want to receive email from your Google+ profile visitors, select the **Allow People to Email You from a Link on Your Profile** checkbox (see Figure 2.12).

FIGURE 2.12   Encourage people to contact you without revealing your email address.

5. From the drop-down list, specify who can view the **Send an Email** button on your profile. See "Specifying Profile Privacy by Section" earlier in this lesson for more information about each option.

6. Click the **Save** button to save your changes.

7. Click the **Done Editing** button at the top of the page.

Specifying the People to Display on Your Profile

When someone visits your Google+ profile, the left column displays photos of the people you share in common, the people in your circles, and the people who have you in their circles. Hovering over someone's photo opens a pop-up box with more information about that person. If you want to restrict who can view your Google+ network or remove this section from your profile completely, you can do so.

To specify the people who display on your profile and who can view them, follow these steps:

1. Click the **Profile** icon at the top of your Google+ page (refer to Figure 2.3).

2. Click the **Edit Profile** button in the upper-right corner of the page.

3. Click the **Change Who Is Visible Here** link at the bottom of the left column of your profile.

4. Verify that the **In Your Circles** and **Have In Your Circles** checkboxes are selected if you want to display these sections on your profile (see Figure 2.13).

In your circles

☑ Show people in

    All circles ▼

Who can see this?
◉ Anyone on the web
○ Your circles

Have you in circles

☑ Show people who have added you to circles

[Save] [Cancel]

FIGURE 2.13   Determine which people display on your profile.

TIP: **You Can Hide This Section on Your Profile**

By default, Google+ displays the people in your circle and the people who have you in circles. To hide this information, remove the checkmarks next to the **In Your Circles** and **Have You in Circles** checkboxes.

---

5. From the drop-down box, select which circles you want to display. You can display people in all circles or only selected circles. For example, you might want to display business associates but not family members.

6. Specify who can see this section on your profile: anyone on the web or only people in your circles.

7. Click the **Save** button to save your changes.

8. Click the **Done Editing** button at the top of the page.

Viewing Your Profile as Others See It

After you finish making edits to your page, you might want to see how your profile changes display to others.

To view your Google+ profile as others see it, follow these steps:

1. Click the **Profile** icon at the top of your Google+ page (refer to Figure 2.3).

2. Click the **View Profile As** button to the right of the profile tabs.

3. Click the **Anyone on the Web** button to view the public version of your profile (see Figure 2.14).

See how your profile appears to others. Type in a name or view as...

Anyone on the web

FIGURE 2.14   You can preview how your profile looks to the world—or to a specific person.

4. If you want to preview how your profile displays to a specific person (such as someone in one of your circles), start typing that person's name in the text box. Google+ searches for and displays matches in your circle. Click the name of a person to view your profile as that person sees it.

5. If your profile displays unexpected results, click the **Edit Profile** button to make profile changes.

6. When you're finished previewing your profile, click the **Done** button.

Adding a Google+ Profile Button to Your Website

If you want to attract more people to your Google+ profile, you can add a Google+ profile button to your website or blog. Adding this button is also a good way to identify site ownership so that your website content displays on the +1's tab of your Google+ profile.

To add a Google+ profile button to your website, follow these steps:

1. Navigate to the Google Profile Button page at http://www.google. com/webmasters/profilebutton, shown in Figure 2.15.

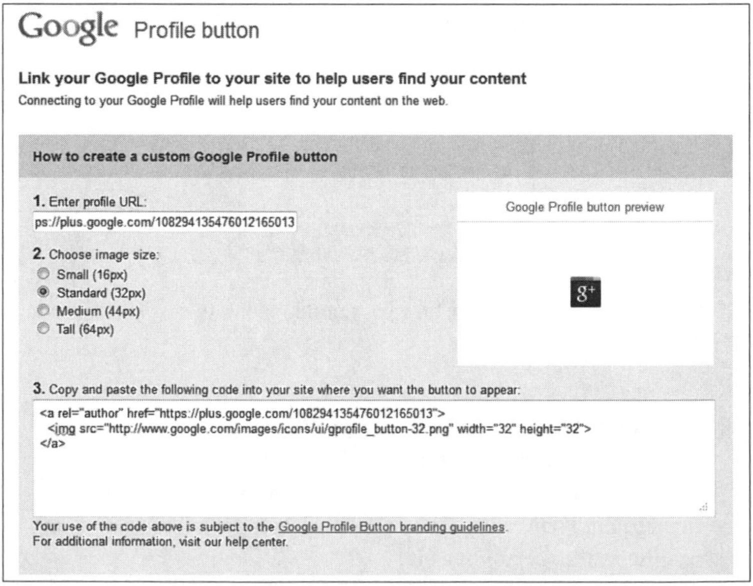

FIGURE 2.15 Let your website or blog visitors know about your Google+ profile.

2. Enter your profile URL in the text box. You can find this by clicking the **[First Name]** link in the upper-left corner of your Google+ home page. Your profile URL is https://plus.google.com plus a 21-digit number. For example, my profile URL is https://plus.google.com/108294135476022165023.

3. Select the image size for your button. Options include small, standard, medium, and tall buttons.

4. Copy and paste the HTML code on your own website or blog.

If you use WordPress, consider adding a googleCard to your sidebar using the googleCards plugin (http://plusdevs.com/google-wordpress-plugin).

Summary

In this lesson, you learned how to edit and manage your profile. Next, it's time to start using Google+ circles.

LESSON 3

Managing Your Network with Circles

In this lesson, you learn how to add and manage Google+ circles.

Understanding Google+ Circles

One of the first things to do when you sign up for Google+ is to add people you know—and those whose posts you find interesting—to circles.

PLAIN ENGLISH: **Google+ Circles**

Circles enable you to organize your Google+ network by placing people into distinct groups. When you post content on Google+, you can specify exactly which circles can view those posts. You can also specify privacy settings by circle. This gives you complete control over who sees what content.

By default, Google+ offers four ready-made circles, but you can also create new circles and delete any circles you don't want to use. The default circles, shown in Figure 3.1, are:

- ▶ **Friends.** People you consider close friends. This circle should be the one you want to give the most access to your Google+ content.

- ▶ **Family.** Family members, including siblings, parents, cousins, and so forth. If what you share with family members varies, consider placing them in separate circles. For example, the content you share with your sister could differ from what you share with your grandmother.

FIGURE 3.1   Google+ gets you started with four ready-made circles.

▶ **Acquaintances.** People you know who aren't close friends or family members. This circle could include co-workers, classmates, or people you know from professional associations, clubs, or community organizations. Creating separate circles for acquaintances based on shared interests is another option. For example, you might create one circle for professional colleagues and another for acquaintances you met through your love for skiing.

▶ **Following.** People whose posts you want to read on Google+, but don't actually know. Celebrities, industry experts, and popular bloggers all fall into this category.

To get started with Google+ circles, you should:

1. Think about how you want to use Google+ and what circles you'll need.

2. Create any new circles.

3. Add people to your circles.

Creating New Circles

When you first start using Google+, you can add people to any of the default circles: Friends, Family, Acquaintances, or Following. Although

these four circles might be sufficient for your needs, you can create other
circles if you want to categorize people further, such as create a circle for
the members of your book club or one for the members of a committee
you are on.

To create a new circle, follow these steps:

1. Click the **Circles** icon at the top of Google+, as shown in
   Figure 3.2.

Circles icon

FIGURE 3.2   Click the Circles icon to access your Google+ circles.

2. Click the **Drop Contacts Here to Create a New Circle** circle in
   the lower-left corner of the page, shown in Figure 3.3.

FIGURE 3.3   You can quickly create new Google+ circles.

3. In the pop-up box that opens (see Figure 3.4), enter a name for
   your circle.

4. If you want to add a description, click the **Click to Add a
   Description** link and enter your content in the text box that displays. You can write a description of up to 350 characters.

5. Optionally, click the **Add a New Person** link to search for people
   to add by name or email address. If you're new to Google+, however, it's easier to create your circles first and then add people to
   them later from the **Find People** tab.

FIGURE 3.4   Give your circle an appropriate name.

6. Click the **Create Empty Circle** button to create your circle and
   close the pop-up box. Your new circle now displays on the
   Circles page, as shown in Figure 3.5.

FIGURE 3.5   You can now add people to your new circle.

Adding People to Circles

When you first sign up for Google+, your circles are empty (refer to Figure
3.2). It's easy to add people to circles, but first you have to find them.
Google+ offers several ways to find people to add to circles. You can:

- ▶ Add people who display on the **Find People** tab on the **Circles**
  page.

- ▶ Add your email contacts.

- ▶ Add people who display in the **Suggestions** section on the right
  side of your Google+ home page.

▶ Add people who appear on your Notifications menu, located in the upper-right corner of the Google+ bar.

▶ Add people from your Incoming stream. See Lesson 6, "Viewing Your Google+ Stream," for more information about this stream.

▶ Add people from their Google+ profile. Many people now display a Google+ button on their website or blog, which makes it easy for you to find their profile.

▶ Send invitations to people who don't use Google+ yet and add them to your circles.

When you add people to circles, Google+ notifies them (on their Notification menu and via email) but doesn't tell them the name of the circle you added them to. For example, if you create an Annoying People circle, no one knows you placed them there.

In addition, adding people to a circle doesn't mean that you are automatically added to their circles. They must take the action to add you to their circles. In this way, adding people to Google+ circles is similar to following people on Twitter. Just because you follow them doesn't mean that they follow you.

Adding People to Circles from the Find People Tab

Discovering people to add to your circles on the **Find People** tab is one of the easiest ways to get started growing your Google+ circles.

To add people from the **Find People** tab, follow these steps:

1. Click the **Circles** icon at the top of Google+ (refer to Figure 3.2).

2. Review the people on the **Find People** tab to locate individuals you want to add to circles. Figure 3.6 shows an example with several people waiting for you to add them to your circles. If the **Email** icon displays in the lower-right corner, this means that the person isn't on Google+. You can share with these people via email or invite them to join Google+.

Email icon

FIGURE 3.6 The **Find People** tab suggests people you might want to add to your circles.

> **NOTE: Why Doesn't Google+ Suggest Any People for Me to Add to Circles?**
>
> If the **Find People** tab doesn't display any people, this means that you haven't added anyone to a circle yet and Google+ couldn't find any email contacts associated with the email address you used to sign up. In this case, follow the other suggestions in this section to search for and add people to your circles. After you have some people in circles, the **Find People** tab will start displaying additional people for you to consider.

3. If the **Find People** tab page contains a large number of people, you can use the **Sort By** drop-down list to sort by first name or last name. By default, Google+ sorts by relevance, placing people who are your direct email contacts at the top of the page.

4. Select and drag people to the appropriate circles using your mouse. If you want to add more than one person to a particular circle, select multiple people and drag the group to the desired circle. You can also add an individual to more than one circle.

Figure 3.7 shows a person added to a circle. On the **Find People** tab, a small circle displays in the lower-right corner of the box surrounding anyone you've added to a circle.

FIGURE 3.7   The people you add to a circle display in that circle's ring.

Understanding Google+ Suggestions

The people Google+ displays on the **Find People** tab come from many sources. These include the following:

▶ People who are in your email address book. Initially, Google+ searches for your contacts using the email address associated with your Google+ account. For example, if you signed up for Google+ with your Gmail address, your Gmail contacts display on the **Find People** tab. You can also search for your Hotmail or Yahoo! Mail contacts or upload an email address book. See "Adding Your Email Contacts" later in this lesson.

▶ People you've interacted with on Google+ or other Google products, including any connected accounts.

▶ People in your extended circles.

> PLAIN ENGLISH: **Extended Circles**
> **Extended Circles** include the people who are in your circles' circles. For example, after you add people to circles, the people in their circles are in your extended circle. Think of them as friends of friends, or friends of the people you follow on Google+.

Deleting People on the Find People Tab

Adding the people Google+ suggests on the **Find People** tab is optional. You can ignore any suggestion or delete the box for that person by pausing over it with your mouse and clicking the **Delete** button (x) in the upper-right corner, as shown in Figure 3.8.

FIGURE 3.8   You can delete suggested people you don't know or don't want to add to a circle.

Adding Your Email Contacts

If the **Find People** tab doesn't display enough people, you can search additional email accounts for more people to add to circles. Google+ enables you to search Yahoo! Mail or Hotmail for contacts or upload your email address book from Outlook, Thunderbird, Apple Address Book, and other email systems.

> NOTE: **Connecting with Your Email Contacts on Google+**
>
> After importing your email contacts, you can add them to your Google+ circles. If they have a Google+ account, they can view your posts on their stream. Otherwise, you can optionally share with them via email or send them an invitation to Google+. To invite an email contact to Google+, double-click this person's name and click the **Invite** button in the **Invite People to Join You on Google+** dialog box, which opens.

Adding Your Hotmail Contacts

If you use Hotmail, you can search for and display your email contacts on the **Find People** tab.

To add your Hotmail contacts to circles, follow these steps:

1. Click the **Circles** icon at the top of Google+ (refer to Figure 3.2).

2. Click the **Hotmail** link on the **Find People** tab, as shown in Figure 3.9.

Orange Hotmail icon

People in your circles (25)   People who've added you (15)   Find people
Sort by: Relevance ▾ Find friends: **Y!** Yahoo!	Hotmail	Upload address book

FIGURE 3.9   Add your Hotmail contacts to the **Find People** tab.

3. In the pop-up box that opens, shown in Figure 3.10, enter your Windows Live ID and password and click the **Connect** button. Google+ connects with Hotmail and displays your email contacts on the **Find People** tab.

FIGURE 3.10   Sign in to Hotmail to give Google+ access to your account.

4. Google+ identifies a Hotmail contact by placing the orange Hotmail icon in the upper-right corner of the box that surrounds that person. Select and drag people to the appropriate circles using your mouse.

Adding Your Yahoo! Mail Contacts

If you use Yahoo! Mail, you can search for and display your email contacts on the **Find People** tab.

To add your Yahoo! Mail contacts to circles, follow these steps:

1. Click the **Circles** icon at the top of Google+ (refer to Figure 3.2).

2. Click the **Yahoo!** link on the **Find People** tab, as shown in Figure 3.11.

Purple Yahoo! icon

FIGURE 3.11   Add your Yahoo! Mail contacts to the **Find People** tab.

3. In the pop-up box that opens, shown in Figure 3.12, enter your Yahoo! ID and password and click the **Sign In** button.

FIGURE 3.12   Sign in to Yahoo! pop-up box.

4. Click the **Agree** button to give Yahoo! permission to share your data. Google+ connects with Yahoo! and displays your email contacts on the **Find People** tab.

5. Google+ identifies a Yahoo! contact by placing the purple **Yahoo!** icon in the upper-right corner of the box that surrounds that person. Select and drag people to the appropriate circles using your mouse.

Adding Email Contacts from an Exported File

If you use another email application—such as Outlook, Thunderbird, or Apple Mail, you can upload and display your email contacts on the **Find People** tab. This process works with any email system that allows you to export your data in either comma-separated values (.csv) or vCard (.vcf) format.

To add your email contacts to circles, follow these steps:

1. Export your email contacts in either .csv or .vcf format following the instructions your email system provides.

2. Click the **Circles** icon at the top of Google+ (refer to Figure 3.2).

3. Click the **Upload Address Book** link on the **Find People** tab. Figure 3.13 shows this link.

FIGURE 3.13 Upload your email contacts to the **Find People** tab.

4. In the **Choose File to Upload** dialog box, select your email contact file and click the **Open** button. Depending on your operating system and browser, the name of this dialog box and button could vary. Google+ uploads your email file and displays your email contacts on the **Find People** tab (see Figure 3.14).

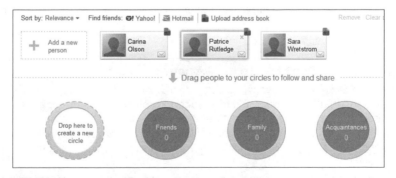

FIGURE 3.14 Add your email contacts to circles.

5. Google+ identifies any uploaded email contact by placing the green file icon in the upper-right corner of the box that surrounds that person. Select and drag people to the appropriate circles using your mouse.

Adding People from the Google+ Suggestions Section

The Google+ Suggestions section on your home page enables you to quickly find and add people to circles.

To add suggested people to circles, follow these steps:

1. Click the **Home** icon at the top of Google+ if you aren't already on the home page. The **Suggestions** section displays in the right column, offering the names and photos of three people Google+ thinks you might want to add to your circles. Figure 3.15 shows a sample Suggestions section.

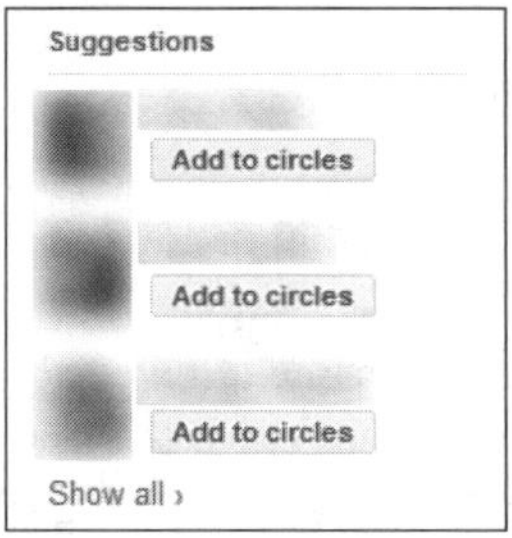

FIGURE 3.15   Google+ suggests three people you might want to add to your circles.

> NOTE: **Why Don't I See a Suggestions Section?**
>
> If the **Suggestions** section doesn't display on your home page, this means that you haven't added anyone to a circle yet and Google+ couldn't find any to suggest. In this case, try another way to search for and add people to your circles. After you have some people in circles, the Suggestions section will start displaying additional people for you to consider.

2. Pause your mouse over the **Add to Circles** button below the name of a person you want to add to a circle. Google+ opens a pop-up box that lists your available circles, as shown in Figure 3.16.

☐ Friends	2
☐ Family	0
☐ Acquaintances	0
☐ Following	0
☐ Business	0
Create new circle	

FIGURE 3.16   Select the right circles for each person you want to add.

3. Select the checkbox to the left of the circle to which you want to add this person. Although you can add people to multiple circles, adding someone to one circle should usually be sufficient. Google+ adds this person to the selected circles and displays a new individual in the Suggestions section.

Optionally, you can

► Add someone to a new circle by clicking the **Create New Circle** link in the pop-up box, typing the name of the new circle, and clicking the **Create** button.

► Remove someone from the **Suggestions** section by pausing the mouse over this person's name and clicking the **Delete** (x) button.

► View additional people by clicking the **Show All** link at the bottom of the Suggestions section. This opens the **Find People** tab.

Add People from the Notifications Menu

You can also add people to circles from the **Notifications** menu. This enables you to see who has added you to their circles and decide whether you want to do the same.

To add people from the **Notifications** menu, follow these steps:

1. Click the **Notifications** button on the Google+ bar that displays in the upper-right corner of the screen, as shown in Figure 3.17.

See Lesson 7, "Using the Google+ Bar," for more information about the features available on this bar.

Notifications button

FIGURE 3.17   Click the **Notifications** button to display a list of your notifications.

2. Click the arrow to the right of the notification to view people associated with it, as shown in Figure 3.18. For example, you can view a list of people who recently added you to their circles.

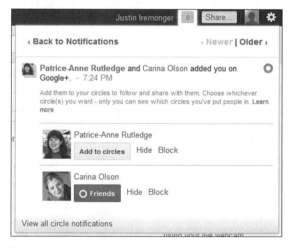

FIGURE 3.18   View people associated with recent notifications.

3. Pause your mouse over the **Add to Circles** button below the name of a person you want to add to a circle. Google+ opens a pop-up box that lists your available circles (refer to Figure 3.16).

4. Select the checkbox to the left of the circle to which you want to add this person and then move your mouse away. Google+ adds this person to the selected circle.

Optionally, you can add someone to a new circle by clicking the **Create New Circle** link in the pop-up box, typing the name of the new circle, and clicking the **Create** button.

Adding People from Your Incoming Stream

Your Incoming stream displays posts from people who have placed you in one of their circles, but aren't in any of your circles yet. See Lesson 6 for more information about the Incoming stream.

To add people from your Incoming stream, follow these steps:

1. Click the **Home** icon at the top of Google+, if you aren't already on your home page.

2. Click the **Incoming** link on the left side of the page to display available posts.

3. Pause your mouse over the **Add to Circles** button to the right of a person you want to add to a circle, as shown in Figure 3.19. Google+ opens a pop-up box that lists your available circles (refer to Figure 3.16).

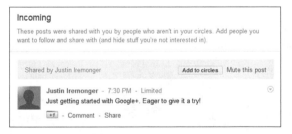

FIGURE 3.19   Add people from the Incoming stream to one of your circles.

4. Select the checkbox to the left of the circle to which you want to add this person. Google+ adds this person to the selected circle.

Adding People from Their Google+ Profile

When you discover Google+ profiles of interesting people, you might want to add them to one of your circles to keep track of what they post.

To add people from their Google+ profiles, follow these steps:

1. Navigate to the Google+ profile of the person you want to add to a circle. You can find profiles by:

   ▶ Searching for someone in the **Find People** box at the top of Google+.

   ▶ Exploring Google+ for interesting people.

   ▶ Searching for someone on Google (www.google.com).

   ▶ Clicking a Google+ button or googleCard on someone's website or blog.

2. Pause your mouse over the **Add to Circles** button in the upper-right corner of the profile whose owner you want to add to a circle, as shown in Figure 3.20. Google+ opens a pop-up box that lists your available circles (refer to Figure 3.16).

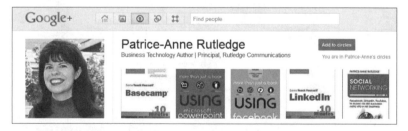

FIGURE 3.20   When you view an interesting Google+ profile, you can add this person to one of your circles.

3. Select the checkbox to the left of the circle to which you want to add this person and then move the mouse away. Google+ adds this person to the selected circle.

Sending Invitations to Friends

If you want to add people to circles who don't use Google+ yet, you can invite them. Google+ allows you to send up to 150 invitations to friends, family, and colleagues.

TIP: **Only Invite People Who Don't Have a Google+ Account**

If someone already has a Google+ account, you should add them to a circle instead of sending an invitation. To find someone's Google+ profile, search for that person in the **Find People** box at the top of the Google+ page.

To send an invitation to Google+, follow these steps:

1. Click the **Home** icon at the top of Google+, if you aren't already on your home page.

2. Click the **Invite Friends** button on the right side of the page, as shown in Figure 3.21.

FIGURE 3.21   Invite people you know to Google+.

3. In the **Invite People to Join You on Google+** pop-up box, click the **+Add People to Invite** link. Figure 3.22 shows this pop-up box.

4. Type the email addresses of the people you want to invite. The **Sign Ups Remaining** box in the lower-right corner lets you know how many invitations you have left.

5. When you finish adding email addresses, click the **Send Email** button.

Invite people to join you on Google+   ✕

Invite people by email.

| + Add people to invite | | Send email |

Or, share this link with a group of people

| https://plus.google.com/_/notifications/ngemlink?path=%2F%3Fgpinv%3DxG8Ps: | 1 5 0 |

Sign ups remaining

FIGURE 3.22   Add one or more people to your invitation list.

6. Optionally, click the **Add to Circles** button next to the name of anyone you want to add to your Google+ circles. Even if they choose not to join Google+, you can share content with them by email. You can also wait to add people to circles after they join Google+.

7. Click the **Done** button when you finish adding people to circles.

Figure 3.23 shows a sample of the email that Google+ sends to people you invite. See Lesson 1, "Introducing Google+," for more information about accepting Google+ invitations.

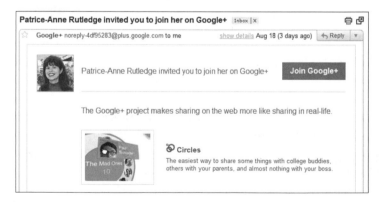

FIGURE 3.23   Google+ sends an email to everyone you invite.

Optionally, you can share the link that displays in the **Invite People to Join You on Google+** pop-up box with a group of people. For example, you could send this link to an existing email group or post it on Facebook, Twitter, or your blog.

Managing Circles

Google+ makes it easy to view and manage the people in your circles. You can move people to other circles, remove individual people from circles, and delete circles.

Viewing People in Your Circles

To view the people in your circles, click the **Circles** icon at the top of Google+ and then click the **People in Your Circles** tab (see Figure 3.24).

FIGURE 3.24   View the people you added to circles.

To arrange the order in which people appear on this tab, select one of the following options from the **Sort By** drop-down list on the left side: First Name, Last Name, Relevance (the default), and Recently Updated.

Viewing People Who Added You to Their Circles

To view the people who have added you to their circles, click the **Circles** icon at the top of Google+ and then click the **People Who've Added You** tab (see Figure 3.25).

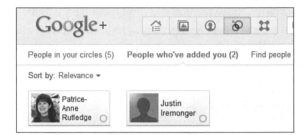

FIGURE 3.25   See who has added you to their circles.

To arrange the order in which people appear on this tab, select one of the following options from the **Sort By** drop-down list on the left side: First Name, Last Name, Relevance (the default), Recently Updated, and Not Yet in Circles.

Moving People from One Circle to Another

If you add someone to the wrong circle or decide you want to rearrange your circles, you can move people easily.

To move someone from one circle to another, follow these steps:

1. Click the **Circles** icon at the top of Google+.

2. Click the **People in Your Circles** tab.

3. Drag the photo of the person you want to move from its existing circle to another circle using your mouse (see Figure 3.26).

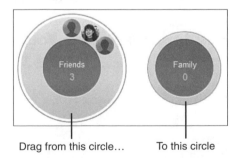

Drag from this circle...   To this circle

FIGURE 3.26   Drag a photo from one circle to another to move that person to another circle.

Removing People from Circles

You can remove people from a circle if you decide you no longer want to view their posts.

To remove someone from a circle, follow these steps:

1. Click the **Circles** icon at the top of Google+.

2. Click the **People in Your Circles** tab.

3. Drag the photo of the person you want to remove away from the circle. Optionally, you can select the box surrounding this person on the top part of the page and click the **Remove** link which is along the top right (see Figure 3.27). Google+ removes the person from the circle.

FIGURE 3.27   Click the **Remove** link to remove the selected person.

CAUTION: **Where Did That Person Go?**

People you remove from a specific circle who are part of other circles remain in those other circles. If you remove people from the only circle they are part of, you remove them entirely from the Circles page. If you change your mind or remove someone by mistake, you need to search for this person again using the **Find People** box at the top of Google+.

Editing a Circle's Name and Description

You can edit the name and description of your circles.

To edit a circle, follow these steps:

1. Click the **Circles** icon at the top of Google+.

2. Right-click the circle you want to edit and select **Edit Circle** from the menu that displays, as shown in Figure 3.28.

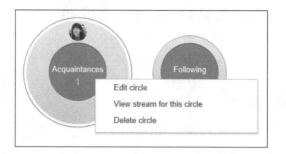

FIGURE 3.28   You can edit any circle's name or description.

3. In the pop-up box that opens (see Figure 3.29), replace the existing name and description with new content.

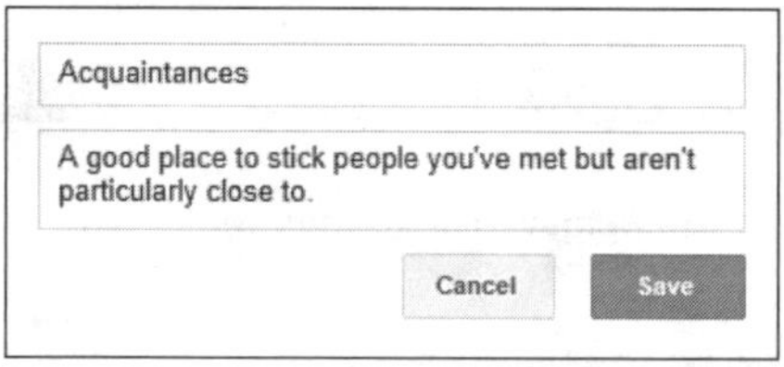

FIGURE 3.29   Edit your circle in this dialog box.

4. Click the **Save** button to save your changes and close the dialog box.

In each circle's dialog box, at the bottom, you can click additional links to view the stream for this circle, view circle members on a tab, or delete the circle.

Deleting a Circle

If you no longer plan to use a circle, or created it by mistake, you can delete it.

To delete a circle, follow these steps:

1. Click the **Circles** icon at the top of Google+.

2. Right-click the circle you want to delete and select **Delete Circle** from the menu that displays (refer to Figure 3.28).

3. In the pop-up box that opens (see Figure 3.30), click the **Delete Circle** button to permanently delete the circle.

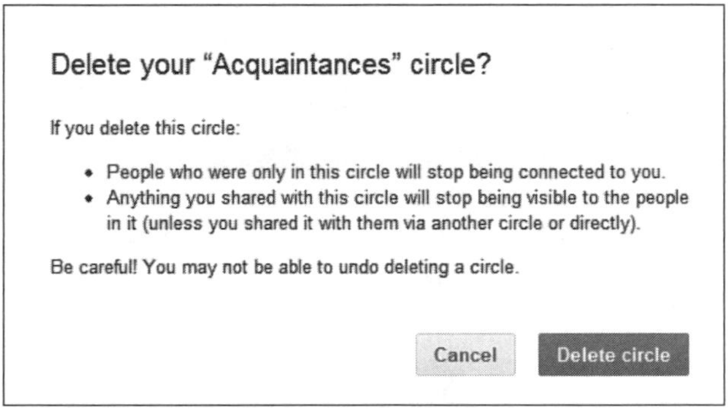

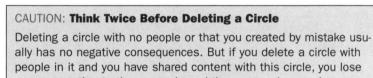

FIGURE 3.30 Delete circles you don't need.

CAUTION: **Think Twice Before Deleting a Circle**

Deleting a circle with no people or that you created by mistake usually has no negative consequences. But if you delete a circle with people in it and you have shared content with this circle, you lose your connection to these people and they can no longer view anything you shared with them. Google+ circle deletions are permanent.

Summary

In this lesson, you learned how to manage your Google+ circles. Next, focus on managing your Google+ privacy settings.

LESSON 4

Managing Google+ Settings and Privacy

In this lesson, you learn how to manage your Google+ account and privacy settings.

Understanding Google+ Privacy

With Google+, you have complete control over who sees your content through a combination of Google+ circles and Google privacy settings. The Google **Accounts** page offers six tabs that enable you to manage your account and privacy settings for Google+ as well as other connected Google products. Before you start sharing content on Google+, you should review the information and settings on this page to ensure that you understand all the available options and make the right choices for your needs.

> TIP: **What Is Google's Privacy Policy for the Content I Share on Google+?**
>
> For a summary of how Google uses and protects your data, read the Google+ Privacy Policy at www.google.com/intl/en/+/policy. This page explains how Google+ uses your data in plain English.

Managing Your Google Account Settings

To manage your Google account settings, click the **Options** button in the upper-right corner of the Google+ bar, select **Google+ Settings** from the drop-down menu, and click the **Account Overview** tab on the Google **Accounts** page. Figure 4.1 shows the location of the **Options** button.

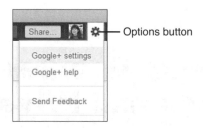

FIGURE 4.1 The **Options** button gives you access to the **Google Accounts** page.

NOTE: **Why Don't I See Google+ Settings on the Menu?**
You must be signed in to Google+ to view **Google+ Settings** on the drop-down menu. If this option isn't available, sign in to Google+ and try again.

On the **Account Overview** tab, shown in Figure 4.2, you can do the following:

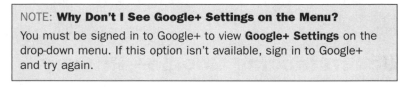

FIGURE 4.2 The **Account Overview** tab provides links to Google pages that help you manage your account.

▶ **Edit your profile.** Click the **Edit Profile** link to open your Google+ profile. See Lesson 2, "Working with Google+ Profiles," for more information about editing your profile.

▶ **Change your password.** Click the **Change Password** link to open the **Change Password** page. To create a secure password, use a combination of uppercase letters, lowercase letters, and numbers. For more password tips, click the **Password Strength** link on this page.

▶ **Change your recovery options.** Click the **Change Recovery Options** link to open the **Recovering Your Password** page. Recovery options enable you to access your account even if you forget your password. Options include password recovery by email, text message, or security question.

▶ **Enable multiple sign-in.** See "Enabling Multiple Sign-In" later in this section for more information.

▶ **Authorize and revoke access to your account.** Click the **Edit** link to the right of the **Authorizing Applications & Sites** field to open the **Authorized Access to Your Google Account** page, shown in Figure 4.3. This page lists all the third-party applications you've authorized to access your Google account, such as Google+ games or other social sites. You can revoke access to any third-party application, but doing so means that your account will no longer be connected. For example, you can no longer play games to which you revoke access.

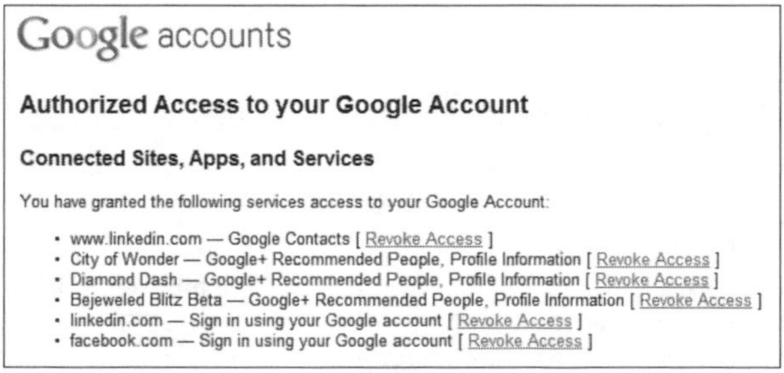

Google accounts

Authorized Access to your Google Account

Connected Sites, Apps, and Services

You have granted the following services access to your Google Account:

- www.linkedin.com — Google Contacts [Revoke Access]
- City of Wonder — Google+ Recommended People, Profile Information [Revoke Access]
- Diamond Dash — Google+ Recommended People, Profile Information [Revoke Access]
- Bejeweled Blitz Beta — Google+ Recommended People, Profile Information [Revoke Access]
- linkedin.com — Sign in using your Google account [Revoke Access]
- facebook.com — Sign in using your Google account [Revoke Access]

FIGURE 4.3   You can revoke access to any third-party applications.

▶ **Enable 2-step verification.** Click the **Edit** link to the right of the Using 2-step Verification field to open the **Protect Your Google Account** page. This feature adds an extra layer of protection to your account but requires that you enter both a password and a verification code each time you sign in.

▶ **Add an alternate email to your account.** Click the **Edit** link in the **Email Addresses** and **Usernames** section, enter an additional email address in the **Add an Alternate Email to Your Account** section, and click the **Save** button. An alternate email address enables you to sign in to your Google account if you can no longer access your primary email account.

▶ **Delete your Google+ profile.** See "Deleting Your Google+ Profile" later in this section for more information.

▶ **Delete your Google account.** See "Deleting Your Google Account" later in this section for more information.

Using Multiple Sign-In

Multiple sign-in enables you to use more than one Google account within the same browser. The following Google products support multiple sign-in: Google+, Calendar, Code, Finance, Gmail, Moderator, iGoogle, News, Reader, Sites, Voice, and Docs. If you switch to a Google product that doesn't support multiple sign-in, it uses the first account you signed into with that browser, not the most recent. In addition, the mobile versions of these products don't support multiple sign-in either.

> NOTE: **Why Should I Enable Multiple Sign-In?**
>
> Multiple sign-in is most useful for people who have more than one Google account or for two or more people who use the same computer. For example, you could have a Google+ account connected to a Gmail account that you use for business and another Gmail account that you use for personal messages and email newsletters. By enabling multiple sign-in, you can access both accounts easily.

Enabling Multiple Sign-In

To enable multiple sign-in, follow these steps:

1. Click the Options button in the upper-right corner of the Google+ bar and select **Google+ Settings** from the drop-down menu.

2. Click the **Account Overview** tab on the Google Accounts page.

3. Click the **Edit** link to the right of the **Multiple Sign-In** field to open the **Sign In to Multiple Accounts** page, shown in Figure 4.4.

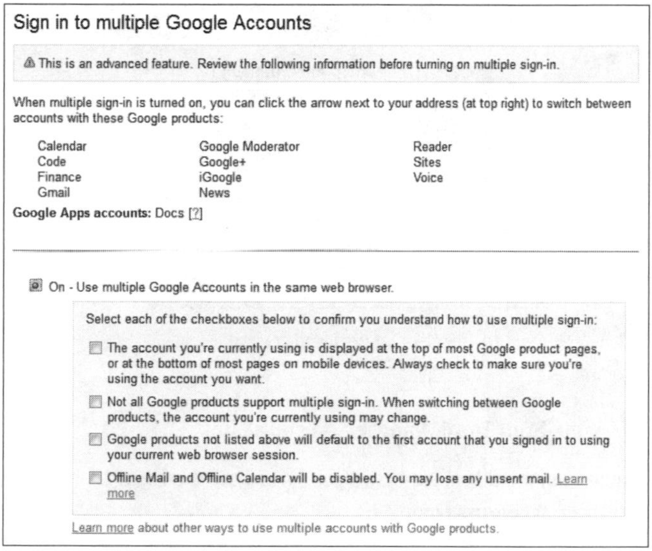

FIGURE 4.4   Working with multiple accounts is easy with Google+.

4. Select the **On** option button.

5. Select the four checkboxes below the **On** option button to confirm that you understand the way multiple sign-in works and affects your accounts. If you need more information about multiple sign-in, click the **Learn More** link.

6. Click the **Save** button.

You can now switch to different accounts when using Google+.

Switching to a Different Account

To switch to a different account from Google+, follow these steps:

1. Click your full name or gravatar in the upper-right corner of the Google+ bar.

2. Click the **Switch Account** link in the pop-up box that opens (see Figure 4.5). This link won't display if you haven't enabled multiple sign-in.

FIGURE 4.5   Switch to another account in Google+.

3. Click the **Sign In to Another Account** link.

4. Enter your email address and password on the **Sign In to Another Account** page.

Google+ switches to that account. While using the same browser session, you can switch between the accounts you're signed in to, as shown in Figure 4.6.

FIGURE 4.6   Switch back and forth between accounts.

Deleting Your Google+ Profile

If you decide you no longer want to maintain your Google+ profile, you can delete it.

> TIP: **Consider Other Options Before Deleting Your Google+ Profile**
>
> If you're thinking about deleting your Google+ profile for privacy concerns, another option is to disable search engine visibility and change the visibility settings for your profile. That way, you can retain a profile but have total control over who can—and can't—view your profile data. See Lesson 2 for more information about editing your profile.

To delete your Google+ profile, follow these steps:

1. Click the **Options** button in the upper-right corner of the Google+ bar and select **Google+ Settings** from the drop-down menu.

2. On the Google Accounts page, select the **Account Overview** tab.

3. At the bottom of the **Account Overview** tab (see Figure 4.7), click the **Delete Profile and Remove Associated Social Features** link.

Services

| Delete profile and social features | Delete profile and remove associated social features |
| Delete account | Close account and delete all services and info associated with it |

FIGURE 4.7   You can delete your Google+ profile if you no longer want to maintain it.

4. On the **Delete Google+ Content or Your Entire Google Profile** page, shown in Figure 4.8, select the **Delete Google+ Content** option button to delete your profile content including circles, posts, and comments, but retain a basic profile for use with Google products that use profile data, such as Google Buzz. Optionally, select the **Delete Your Entire Google Profile** option button to delete circles, posts, comments, and your profile.

5. Check the box stating that you understand that deleting this service can't be undone and the data deleted can't be restored.

FIGURE 4.8   Delete your Google+ content or your entire profile.

6. Click the **Remove Selected Services** button and confirm your deletion.

Deleting Your Google Account

Another option is to delete your entire Google account, which removes access to all Google products, including Google+.

CAUTION: **Think Twice Before Deleting Your Google Account**

Deleting your Google account doesn't just delete your Google+ profile. It also deletes your account on any other Google products you have, such as Gmail, Google Reader, Google Buzz, Google Checkout, and more. Be very sure that you really want to delete *everything* before proceeding with this option. If privacy is your concern, this lesson offers many suggestions for protecting your privacy while still maintaining your accounts.

To delete your Google account, follow these steps:

1. Click the **Options** button in the upper-right corner of the Google+ bar and select **Google+ Settings** from the drop-down menu.

2. On the Google Accounts page, select the **Account Overview** tab.

3. At the bottom of the Account Overview tab (refer to Figure 4.7), click the **Close Account and Delete All Services and Info Associated with It** link to open the **Delete Google Account** page

(see Figure 4.9). This is a powerful page; it enables you to delete your accounts for *all* Google products.

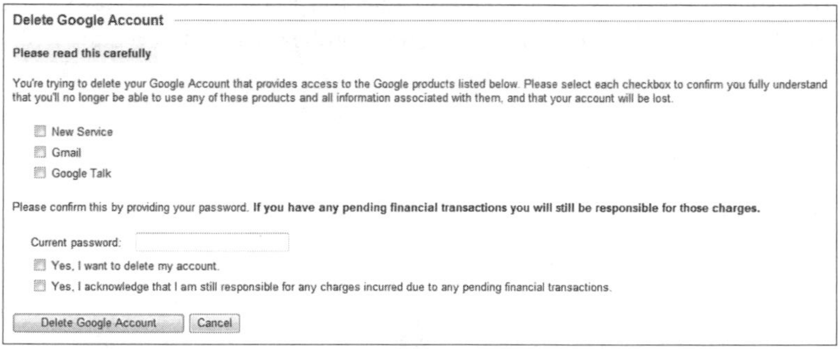

Delete Google Account

Please read this carefully

You're trying to delete your Google Account that provides access to the Google products listed below. Please select each checkbox to confirm you fully understand that you'll no longer be able to use any of these products and all information associated with them, and that your account will be lost.

☐ New Service
☐ Gmail
☐ Google Talk

Please confirm this by providing your password. **If you have any pending financial transactions you will still be responsible for those charges.**

Current password: [   ]

☐ Yes, I want to delete my account.
☐ Yes, I acknowledge that I am still responsible for any charges incurred due to any pending financial transactions.

[Delete Google Account] [Cancel]

FIGURE 4.9   Be sure that you really want to delete your entire Google account before proceeding.

4. Select the checkbox next to each Google product that displays on this page. This confirms that you understand Google will delete your account on these products and you can no longer use them. You can't select only certain checkboxes; you must select them all to confirm you really want to delete all Google products.

5. Confirm your password.

6. Confirm that you want to delete your account and that you understand that you're still responsible for any pending financial transactions (for example, using Google Checkout) by selecting the corresponding checkboxes.

7. Click the **Delete Google Account** button and confirm the permanent deletion of your account.

Managing Your Privacy Settings

To manage your privacy settings, click the **Options** button in the upper-right corner of the Google+ bar, select **Google+ Settings** from the drop-down menu, and click the **Profile and Privacy** tab on the Google **Accounts** page.

Managing Privacy Settings for Your Google+ Profile

The **Google Profiles** section on the **Profile and Privacy** tab previews what your Google+ profile looks like in search results, as shown in Figure 4.10.

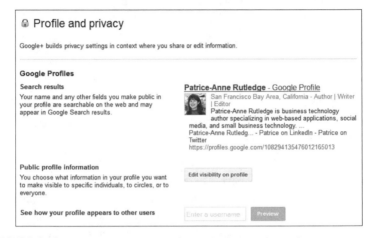

FIGURE 4.10   Preview how your profile looks in search results.

To edit your profile visibility, click the **Edit Visibility on Profile** button to open your profile in Edit mode. For example, you can specify privacy settings for each section of your profile and choose whether or not to make your profile visible in search engine results. See Lesson 2 for more information about editing your profile.

If you want to preview how your profile looks to a certain person, enter that person's name in the text box and click the **Preview** button on the **Profile and Privacy** page. Google+ displays your profile exactly as the named person would see it. For example, you might want to preview how your profile looks to your parents, your boss, and so forth if you use Google+ to communicate with multiple audiences such as family, friends, and work colleagues.

Managing Google+ Sharing

The **Sharing** section of the **Profile and Privacy** page, shown in Figure 4.11, helps you manage the privacy of the content you share on Google+.

Sharing

Circles

Circles are groups of people you share content with. The names of your circles and who you add to them are visible only to you, though you can set whether the list of people in all of your circles is visible in your public profile.

Manage circles

Network Visibility

You can control which people appear on your profile. Note that circle names are never revealed.

Edit network visibility

Who can share posts with you

Anyone can share a post with you, but your stream only includes posts from people you've added to your circles. Click Incoming to see what people who aren't in your circles want to share with you.

View incoming posts

Who posts are shared with

Each post has an indicator that summarizes who the post is shared with (Public, Limited, and so on). Click the indicator for details about who the post is shared with. Remember that anyone a post is shared with can see all comments to that post, who else it's shared with, and share the post with others.

Sharing defaults

Each time you post content, you specify the circles and individuals you want to share it with. For convenience, new posts default to the last set of people you shared a post with, but you can change that before you post.

FIGURE 4.11   Learn more about how sharing works in Google+.

This section provides information about Google+ sharing all in one place with tips, information, and links to other areas of Google+ where you can specify your sharing preferences. In this section, you can:

▶ Click the **Manage Circles** button to open the **Circles** page where you can place people in circles that determine what content they can view. See Lesson 3, "Managing Your Network with Circles," for more information about how circles help you manage the way you share with others.

▶ Click the **Edit Network Visibility** button to open the **About** tab on your profile where you can disable search engine visibility if you don't want anyone to find your profile on a search engine such as Google, Yahoo!, or Bing. See Lesson 2 for more information about profile privacy.

► Click the **View Incoming Posts** button to view incoming posts from people who aren't in your circles but have placed you in one of their circles. See Lesson 6, "Viewing Your Google+ Stream," for more information about viewing posts on the Incoming stream.

Managing Other Google+ Options

Figure 4.12 shows the **Google+** section of the **Profile and Privacy** tab.

Google+

Photos
You can specify who can automatically tag you with a tag linked to your Google Profile, whether to attach the location where you took photos when you upload them, and whether to include a Photos tab in your public profile.

[Edit photos settings]

Sparks
Only you can see the interests you follow in Sparks.

[Edit interests]

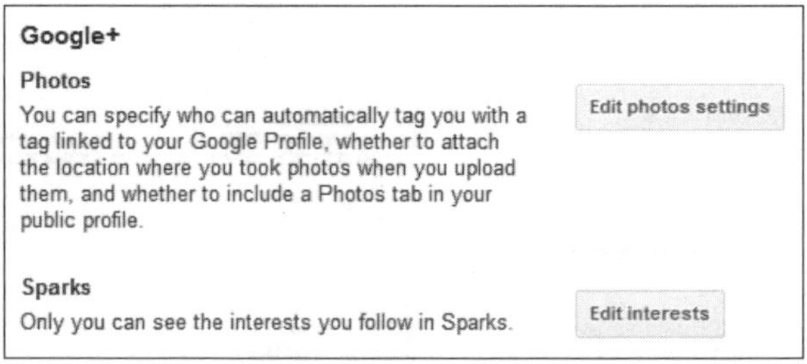

FIGURE 4.12   Specify privacy settings for other Google+ features such as photos and interests.

In this section, you can:

► Click the **Edit Photos Settings** button to open the **Photos** section of the Google+ tab where you can manage your photo settings. See Lesson 8, "Working with Photos," for more information.

► Click the **Edit Interests** button to open the Google+ search page, where you can search for web content related to your interests.

Managing Google Privacy Options

The **Google Privacy** section of the **Profile and Privacy** tab, shown in Figure 4.13, leads you to other areas of Google where you can manage your Google products and learn more about privacy options.

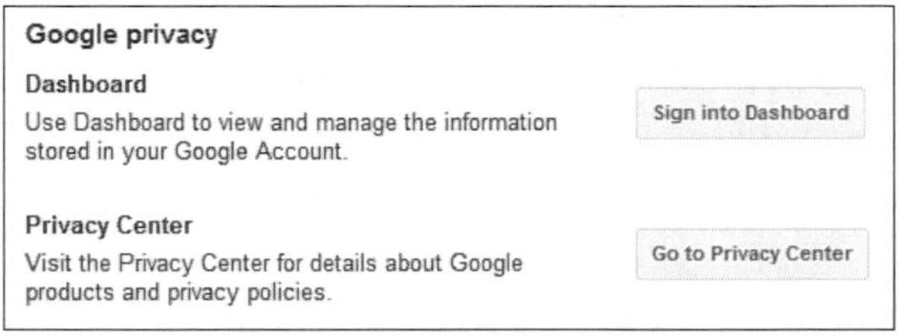

Google privacy

Dashboard
Use Dashboard to view and manage the information
stored in your Google Account.

Sign into Dashboard

Privacy Center
Visit the Privacy Center for details about Google
products and privacy policies.

Go to Privacy Center

FIGURE 4.13   Click the **Go to Privacy Center** button to learn more about
your privacy options.

In this section, you can:

- ▶ Click the **Sign Into Dashboard** button to sign into your Google
  Dashboard. On the Dashboard, you can manage all your Google
  products, including Google+, Gmail, Docs, Talk, Buzz, and more.

- ▶ Click the **Go to Privacy Center** button to open the **Google
  Privacy Center** page, which includes information and videos
  about protecting your privacy.

Managing Google+ Settings

To manage your Google+ settings, click the **Options** button in the upper-
right corner of the Google+ bar, select **Google+ Settings** from the drop-
down menu, and click the **Google+** tab on the **Google Accounts** page.
Figure 4.14 shows the Google+ tab.

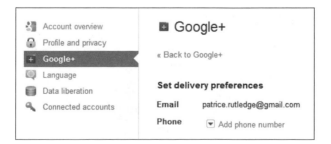

FIGURE 4.14   Specify how you want Google+ to notify you on the Google+
tab.

On this tab, you can set your email and phone delivery preferences, set your notification preferences, and specify +1 personalization.

This tab also offers several fields for specifying photo preferences. See Lesson 8 for more information about these preferences.

Setting Delivery Preferences

The **Set Delivery Preferences** section of the Google+ tab displays the email address and mobile phone number where you want to receive notifications. You can change your email address on the **Account Overview** tab. If you haven't connected a mobile phone to this account, you can do so on this tab.

To add a phone number, follow these steps:

1. Click the **Add Phone Number** link in the **Set Delivery Preferences** section of the Google+ tab (refer to Figure 4.14).

2. Enter your country and phone number.

3. Click the **Send Verification Code** button. Google+ sends a verification code by text message to your phone.

4. Enter your six-digit code in the **Verification Code** field, shown in Figure 4.15, and click the **Confirm** button.

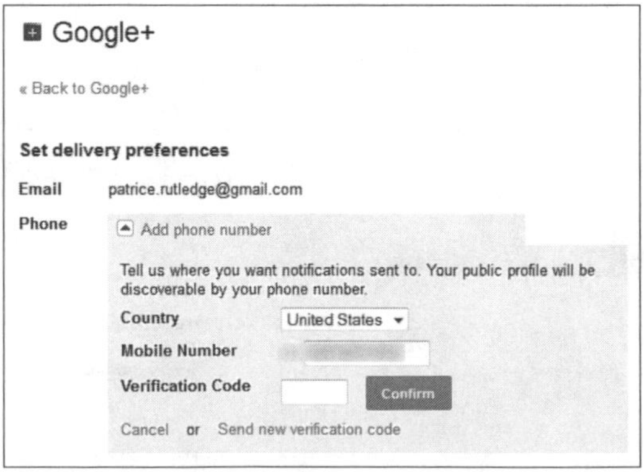

FIGURE 4.15   Enter the verification code you receive by text message.

5. Select the **SMS** option button if you want to receive selected Google+ notifications by text message. Select the **Don't Notify Me** option button if you don't want to receive text message notifications. Figure 4.16 shows these option buttons.

FIGURE 4.16 Specify whether or not you want to receive notifications by SMS.

Be sure to specify your notification preferences after enabling SMS so that you can control the volume of messages you receive.

Specify Notification Preferences

The **Receive Notifications** section of the **Google+** tab enables you to specify which actions trigger a Google+ notification and how to send this notification: by email, via SMS text message, or both.

Figure 4.17 shows the **Receive Notifications** section, which displays the events that trigger notifications, such as when someone mentions you in a post, adds you to a circle, tags you, comments on one of your posts, starts a Huddle conversation with you, and so forth.

For each event, you can select your preferred notification method. If you don't want to receive any notifications, remove the checkmarks from all checkboxes.

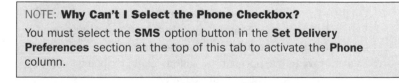

NOTE: **Why Can't I Select the Phone Checkbox?**
You must select the **SMS** option button in the **Set Delivery Preferences** section at the top of this tab to activate the **Phone** column.

Receive notifications		
Get notified by email or SMS when someone...		
Posts and mentions of my name	✉ Email	📱 Phone
Mentions me in a post	☑	☐
Shares a post with me directly	☑	☐
Comments on a post I created	☑	☐
Comments on a post after I comment on it	☑	☐
Circles	✉ Email	📱 Phone
Adds me to a circle	☑	☐
Photos of me	✉ Email	📱 Phone
Wants to tag me in a photo	☑	☐
Tags me in a photo	☑	☐
Comments on a photo after I comment on it	☑	☐
Comments on a photo I am tagged in	☑	☐
Comments on a photo I tagged	☑	☐
Huddle	✉ Email	📱 Phone
Starts a Huddle conversation with me	☑	☑

FIGURE 4.17   You have control over which notifications you receive and how you receive them.

Enabling +1 Personalization

By default, Google+ disables +1 personalization on third-party sites, but you can enable this feature if you want to. When you enable +1 personalization, Google uses your account data, such as the names of people in your circles, to personalize content and ads on third-party sites. For example, you could see the name of someone in one of your circles who has clicked the +1 button to show support for a post on a popular website.

To enable this feature, follow these steps:

1. Click the **Edit** link in the **Google +1** section on the **Google+** tab.

2. On the **+1 Personalization on Non-Google Sites** page, shown in Figure 4.18, select the **Enable** option button. If you want to read more information about the ramifications of this choice, click the **Learn More** link to open a page with a detailed explanation of +1 personalization with several examples.

3. Click the **Save** button.

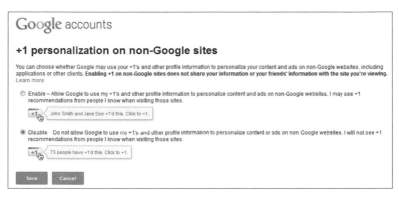

FIGURE 4.18 Decide whether or not you want to enable +1 personalization.

Specifying Your Preferred Languages

Google enables you to view its products in multiple languages. For example, you can view Google+ in more than 40 languages ranging from Arabic to Vietnamese. Because Google hasn't localized all its products in every language it supports, you can specify secondary languages if your primary language isn't available for a specific product.

To specify your preferred languages, follow these steps:

1. Click the **Options** button in the upper-right corner of the Google+ bar (refer to Figure 4.1).

2. Select **Google+ Settings** from the drop-down menu.

3. Click the **Language** tab on the **Google Accounts** page.

4. Select your default language from the **Primary Language** drop-down list (see Figure 4.19). This field displays the current language you're using to view the Google+ interface, but you can choose from dozens of other languages. For example, if you're currently viewing Google+ in English but would rather view it in Italian, select Italian as your primary language.

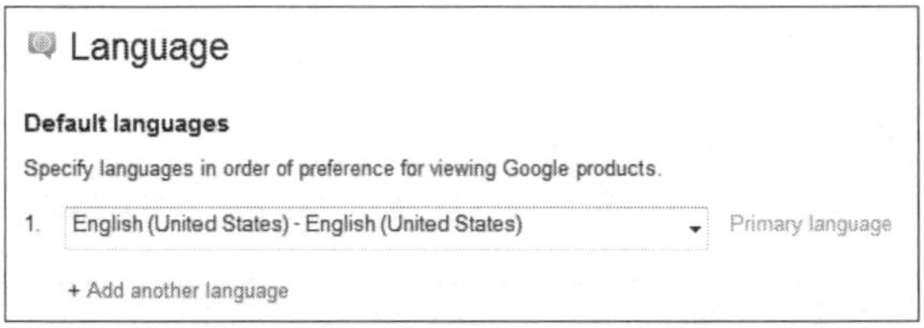

FIGURE 4.19   View Google+ in your preferred language.

5. If you changed your default language in Step 4, click the **Reload** link in the Google+ bar to switch languages. Figure 4.20 shows Google+ in Italian. Be aware that although Google localizes the Google+ product interface, user content such as posts and comments remain in their original language.

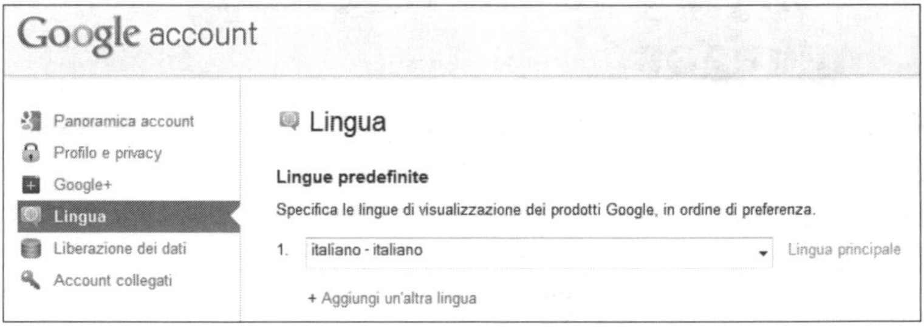

FIGURE 4.20   Google+ is available in more than 40 languages, including Italian.

6. Optionally, click the **Add Another Language** link to add a second language to this list (see Figure 4.21). This option is useful if you would like to view Google products in another language you know when your native language isn't available. For example, if you're a native speaker of Estonian but also speak English, you should list Estonian first and then English.

You can change a secondary language to your primary language by clicking the **Make Primary** link to its right. You can also delete a language by clicking the **Remove** link to its right. You can change your primary language, but you can't delete it.

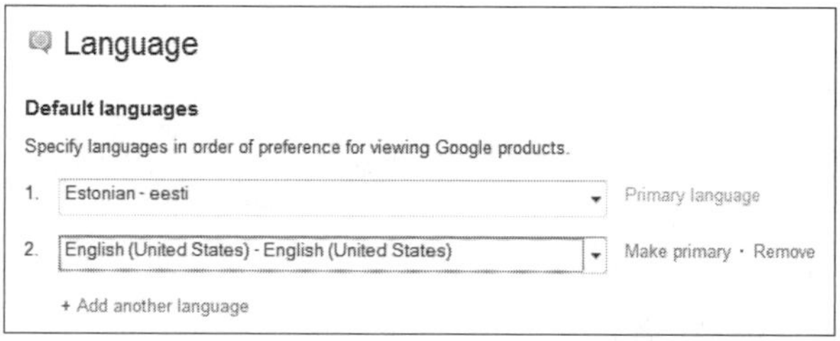

FIGURE 4.21   If Google products aren't available in your primary language, you can specify one or more secondary languages.

Backing Up Your Data

Google enables you to back up your critical data using Google Takeout, which creates a downloadable archive of your +1s, Buzz content, contacts, Picasa web albums, and Google+ profile, circles, and stream. You can download all your Google data or only specific data.

To download your Google data, follow these steps:

1. Click the **Options** button in the upper-right corner of the Google+ bar and select **Google+ Settings** from the drop-down menu.

2. On the **Google Accounts** page, select the **Data Liberation** tab, as shown in Figure 4.22.

3. Click the **Download Your Data** button. Optionally, you can click one of the five links that display at the bottom of the page to download only specific data.

4. Confirm your password to verify your identity.

5. On the **Takeout** page (see Figure 4.23), click the **All of Your Data** tab. Optionally, click the **Choose Services** tab and select from the available download options: +1s, Buzz, Contacts and Circles, Picasa Web Albums, Profile, or Stream.

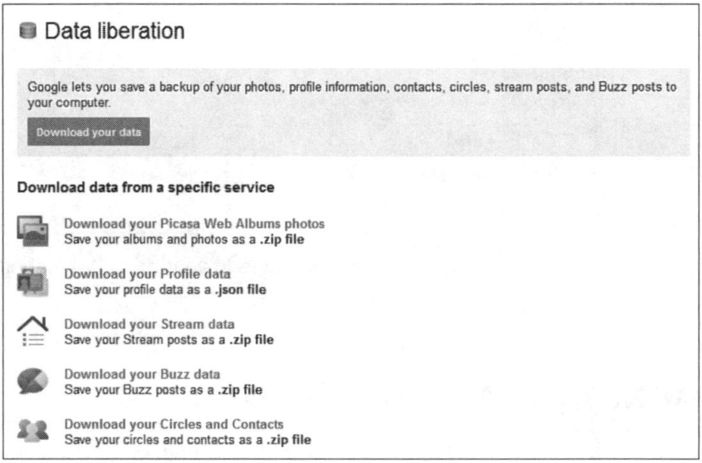

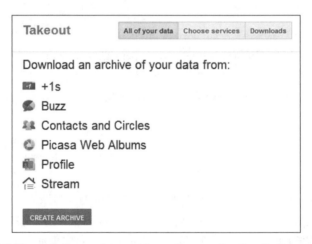

FIGURE 4.22   Back up your Google+ data for safekeeping.

> **Takeout**   All of your data | Choose services | Downloads
>
> ### Download an archive of your data from:
>
> +1s
>
> Buzz
>
> Contacts and Circles
>
> Picasa Web Albums
>
> Profile
>
> Stream
>
> CREATE ARCHIVE

FIGURE 4.23   Select your data archive options on the **Google Takeout** page.

6. Click the **Create Archive** button. Google+ analyzes your data and displays a summary on the **Downloads** tab, as shown in Figure 4.24. Your download is available for one week.

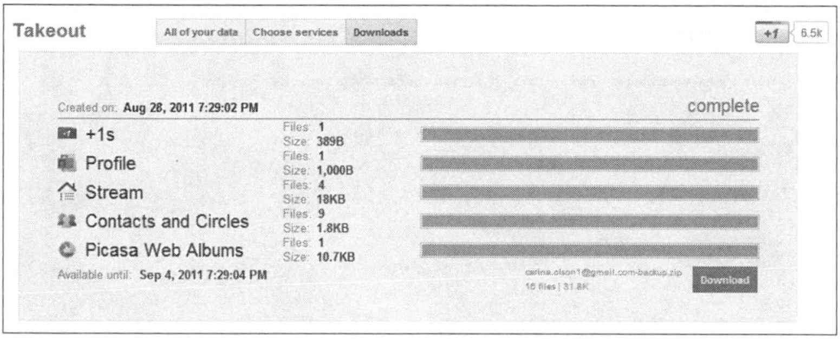

FIGURE 4.24 The **Downloads** tab summarizes your data archive.

7. Click the **Download** button in the lower-right corner. Google prompts you to save your download file to your computer. The exact process for this varies by operating system and browser.

Google places a .zip file in your default **Downloads** folder, or in a folder you specify, using the following naming convention: [email address]-backup.zip. You can store this file for safekeeping or unzip it for another use, such as managing downloaded photos in an external photo album.

Managing Your Connected Accounts

To manage your Google+ connected accounts, click the **Options** button in the upper-right corner of the Google+ bar, select **Google+ Settings** from the drop-down menu, and click the **Connected Accounts** tab on the Google Accounts page.

Figure 4.25 shows this tab, which displays the accounts you're already connected to. For example, any sites you added to the Links section of your profile display here.

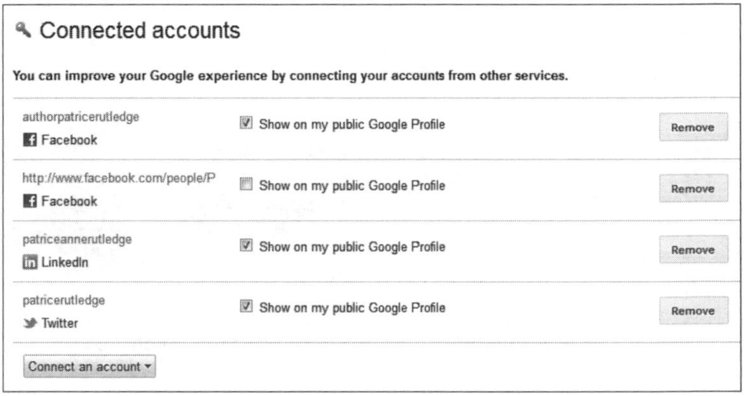

FIGURE 4.25   Manage which connected accounts you display on your profile.

Showing Connected Account Links on Your Google+ Profile

Select the **Show on My Public Google Profile** checkbox for any site you want to list in the **Links** section on your profile (refer to Figure 4.25). Optionally, you can remove any connected account by clicking the **Remove** button to its right.

Connecting More Accounts

You can connect more external accounts to your Google+ account.

To connect another account, follow these steps:

1. Click the **Connect an Account** button and select one of the available options from the drop-down list: Facebook, Yahoo!, Flickr, LinkedIn, Quora, Twitter, Yelp, Hotmail, MySpace, or Plaxo.

2. Enter your account URL for that site, as shown in Figure 4.26.

3. Click the **Add** button.

4. Optionally, click the **Show on My Public Google Profile** checkbox.

authorpatricerutledge **f** Facebook	☑ Show on my public Google Profile	Remove
http://www.facebook.com/people/P **f** Facebook	☐ Show on my public Google Profile	Remove
patriceannerutledge **in** LinkedIn	☑ Show on my public Google Profile	Remove
patricerutledge **y** Twitter	☑ Show on my public Google Profile	Remove
Quora ▾	Account Name or Profile Link ☐ Add this link to my public Google Profile, too	Add

FIGURE 4.26   Connect additional accounts to Google+.

Allowing Google+ to Search for Connected Accounts

By default, Google searches for your accounts on other social sites using your personal information, such as your email address. If you don't want Google to do this, at the bottom of the **Connected Accounts** page, remove the checkmark from the **Use My Google Contact Information to Suggest Accounts from Other Sites** checkbox.

Summary

In this lesson, you learned how to manage your Google+ account and privacy settings. Next, get started sharing some content on Google+.

LESSON 5

Sharing Content on Google+

In this lesson, you learn how to share content on Google+, including photos, videos, and links.

Using the Share Box

The share box displays at the top of your Google+ home page, ready for you to share interesting content with your friends and colleagues—or everyone on the web. Using the share box, you can share text updates, links, photos, videos, and even your location.

To share a post using the share box, follow these steps:

1. Click the **Home** icon at the top of Google+ if you aren't already on your home page. Figure 5.1 displays your Google+ stream, which opens. Your stream enables you to share content as well as view content other people have shared. See Lesson 6, "Viewing Your Google+ Stream," for more information.

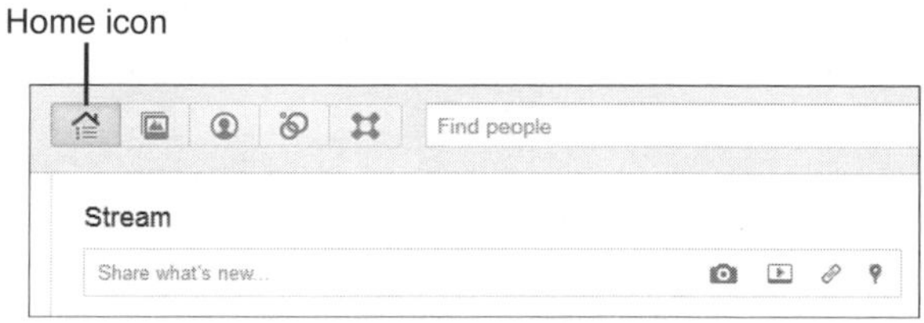

Home icon

FIGURE 5.1 Click the Home icon to access the share box on your Google+ stream.

> TIP: **Access the Share Box from the Google+ Bar**
>
> Another way to access the share box is from the Google+ bar. Click the **Share** button in the upper-right corner of the Google+ bar to open it. This feature is most useful when you're on a Google site other than Google+ and want to share something. See Lesson 7, "Using the Google+ Bar," for more information about this bar.

2. Click in the share box to expand it, as shown in Figure 5.2.

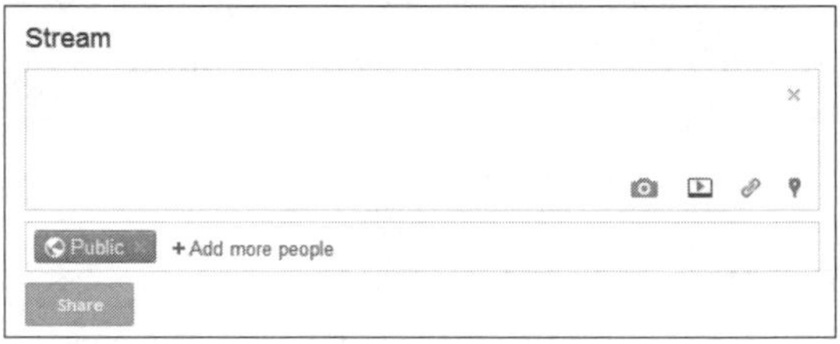

Stream

FIGURE 5.2   Expand the share box to display additional fields.

3. Type your post in the text box.

4. Optionally, you can add other content and apply formatting to your posts. These tasks are covered later in this lesson. For example, you can do the following:

> ▶ Format your post using bolding and italics.
>
> ▶ Add a link to the profile of another Google+ user you mention.
>
> ▶ Add a photo.
>
> ▶ Add a video.
>
> ▶ Add a link to an external website.
>
> ▶ Share your location.

5. Specify who you want to share this post with. Your options include:

> ▶ **Anyone on the web.** By default, Google+ makes your initial post public, visible to anyone on the web. Later,

Google+ uses the default settings from your most recent post. If you don't want to share this post publicly, click the **Delete** icon (x) on the right side of the **Public** chip.

▶ **People in specific circles.** To share this post with specific circles, click the **Add More People** link. In the menu that opens (see Figure 5.3), select the circles you want to share with. If you want to share with all your circles, select **Your Circles**. If you want to share with your extended circles (friends of friends), select **Extended Circles**. When you're finished selecting circles, click outside the menu to close it.

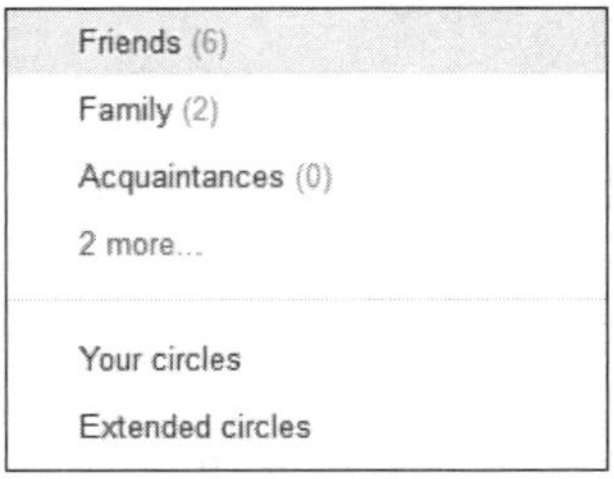

Friends (6)

Family (2)

Acquaintances (0)

2 more...

Your circles

Extended circles

FIGURE 5.3   You can choose the specific circles you want to share with.

▶ **A specific person.** This is the equivalent of sending a private message on Google+. If the person you want to share with uses Google+, type the person's name in the text box and select from the pop-up menu of potential matches (see Figure 5.4). Optionally, you can enter an email address to share with someone who doesn't use Google+ yet.

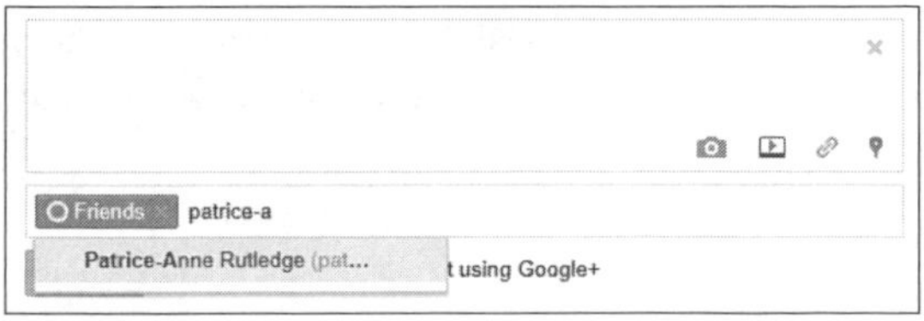

Friends   patrice-a

Patrice-Anne Rutledge (pat...   t using Google+

FIGURE 5.4   You can share a post with just one person.

NOTE: **Understanding Color-Coded Sharing Chips**

Google+ uses color-coded chips to differentiate the groups of people you share with. The **Public** and **Extended Circles** chips are green, which signifies that you are sharing with people you don't know. The chips corresponding to your own circles or individual people are blue, which signifies that you are sharing with people you know.

6. If you want to send a notification and email message about this post to the people in a circle, hover the mouse above that circle and select the **Notify About This Post** checkbox. In general, you should send notifications and emails only for very urgent or important posts.

7. If any of the people in your selected circles aren't on Google+ yet, click the following link to send them your post by email instead: **Also Email [Number of] People Not Yet Using Google+**. For example, if two people you added to circles haven't signed up for Google+ yet, this link says "2 People." Again, use caution when emailing people and send emails only for very important content.

NOTE: **Who Will Receive an Email?**

To view a list of the people who will receive this email, click the **[Number of] People** link. A pop-up box displays the people in your circles who aren't on Google+ yet.

8. Click the **Share** button to share your post with the people you selected.

Figure 5.5 shows a sample post, visible on the streams of the people you shared with as well as on your public profile if you selected to make this post public.

FIGURE 5.5   A post shared on Google+.

After you share a post:

▶ You can edit its content, delete it, or prevent others from sharing
   or commenting on it.

▶ Your Google+ network can comment on, share, or +1 this post.

See Lesson 6 for more information about these tasks and features.

Formatting Your Posts

Google+ enables you to format your posts using bolding, italics, and
strikethroughs. You can:

▶ Bold text by surrounding it with asterisks.

▶ Italicize text by surrounding it with underscore.

▶ Strike through text by surrounding it with hyphens.

Figure 5.6 shows an example of formatting text in the share box.

Figure 5.7 shows an example of the results of this formatting.

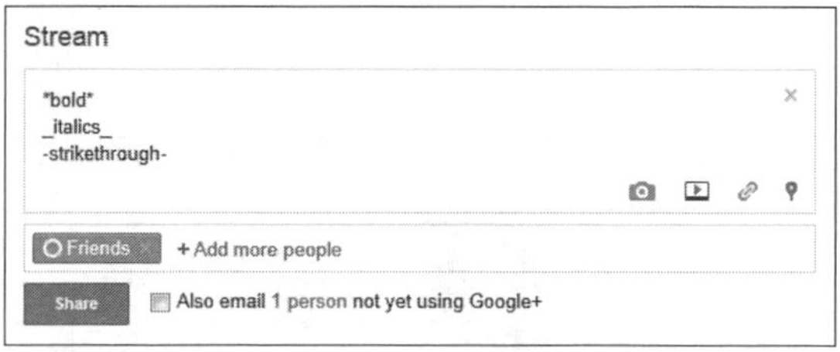

```
Stream

*bold*                                               ×
_italics_
-strikethrough-

                                   📷  ▣  ✑  ⚲

 ◯ Friends ×   + Add more people

    Share       ☐ Also email 1 person not yet using Google+
```

FIGURE 5.6   Use these characters to apply text formatting to your posts.

Carina Olson - 12:47 PM - Limited
bold
italics
~~strikethrough~~

+1 - Comment - Share

FIGURE 5.7   Formatting in a live post.

Mentioning Other People in Your Posts

When you mention another Google+ user in a post, you can link to that person's Google+ profile. Mentioning a person is most useful when you want to give someone public credit or thanks within the Google+ community. Google+ also notifies this person of the mention.

To mention someone in a post, enter the plus sign (+) or at sign (@) in the share box, start typing someone's name, and select the person you want to mention, as shown in Figure 5.8.

FIGURE 5.8   Select the person you want to mention from the list of Google+ users.

Figure 5.9 shows a sample mention in a published post. You can pause your mouse over a mention to view a pop-up box with more information or click the mentioned name to view this person's Google+ profile.

FIGURE 5.9   Pause your mouse over a mention to view a pop-up box.

Sharing Your Location

Optionally, you can share your location in your Google+ post.

To share your location, click the **Add Your Location** button in the lower-right corner of the share box, shown in Figure 5.10. Google+ analyzes your location and displays it at the bottom of your post.

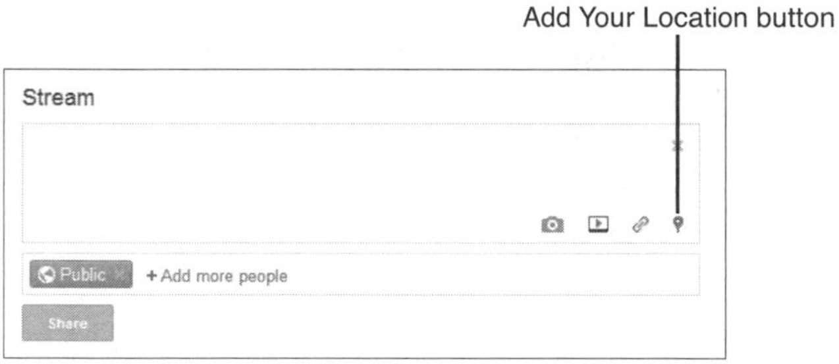

Add Your Location button

Stream

○ Public ∨ + Add more people

Share

FIGURE 5.10   You can display your location in your Google+ posts, but consider carefully whom you want to share this information with.

CAUTION: **Think Twice Before Sharing Your Location**

The Google+ location-sharing feature is most useful when you're away from home and want to share your location from a mobile device. For example, you could let the people in one of your circles know that you're at an event or a favorite restaurant. Be careful using this feature from your home computer as Google+ could display your home address on your post.

Sharing Photos

You can easily share photos on your Google+ posts. For example, you could share vacation photos only with your Friends and Family circles or photos of your company's products on a public post. Google+ offers unlimited photo uploads. If your photos are larger than 2,048 by 2,048 pixels, however, Google+ resizes them during the upload process.

See Lesson 8, "Working with Photos," for more information about the many ways you can use photos in Google+.

To share a photo on Google+, follow these steps:

1. Click the **Home** icon at the top of Google+ if you aren't already on your home page (refer to Figure 5.1).

2. Click in the share box to expand it (refer to Figure 5.2).

3. Type your post in the text box. For example, you can introduce or comment on the photo you're sharing.

4. Click the **Add Photos** button in the lower-right corner of the share box. A pop-up menu opens, offering three ways to add photos (see Figure 5.11).

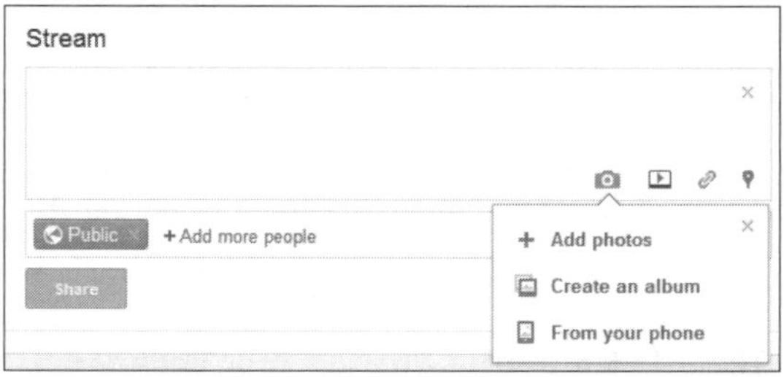

FIGURE 5.11   Add photos to enliven your posts.

5. Attach your photo to the post by selecting one of the following menu options:

   ► **Add Photos.** Search for and upload a photo from your computer. Using this method, you can add only one photo at a time. To add more photos, click the **Add More** link (see Figure 5.12). If you want to add a caption or rotate your photo, click the **Edit Photos** link. To delete a photo, click the **Delete** button (x) in its upper-right corner.

   ► **Create an Album.** Create and upload a photo album by selecting multiple photos from your computer. Figure 5.13 shows the **Create an Album** dialog box, which opens. See Lesson 8 for more information about photo albums.

Edit photos - Add more

FIGURE 5.12   You can edit your photo or add more photos to your post.

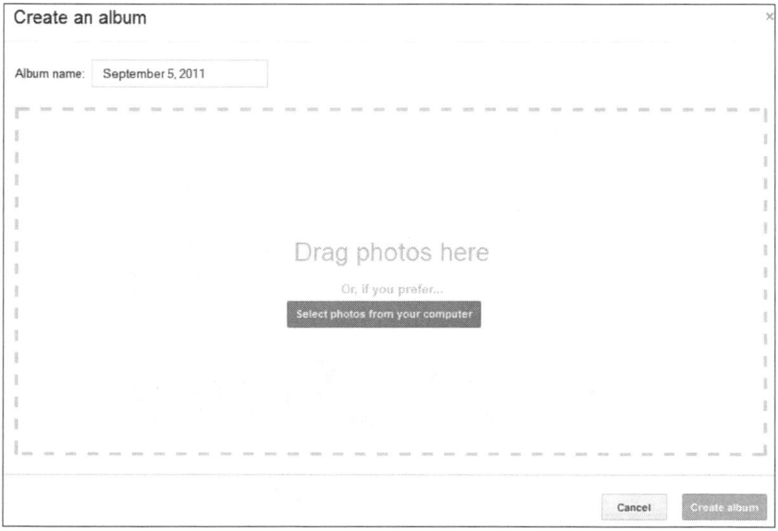

Create an album   ×

Album name: September 5, 2011

Drag photos here

Or, if you prefer...

Select photos from your computer

Cancel   Create album

FIGURE 5.13   Post multiple photos in an album.

▶ **From Your Phone.** Upload photos from your phone. You
  must have an Android 2.1+ smartphone and download the
  Google+ for Android app to use this feature. Google+
  uploads the photos you take from your phone and places

them on the **Photos from Your Phone** tab on the **Photos** page. These photos remain private until you choose to share them. See https://market.android.com/details?id=com.google.android.apps.plus&hl=en for more information about this app.

6. Select the people or circles you want to share this post with or, optionally, make this post public. For a reminder of how to do this, refer to steps 5 through 7 in the section "Using the Share Box" earlier in this lesson.

7. Click the **Share** button to share your post with the people you selected.

Figure 5.14 shows a sample post with a photo.

FIGURE 5.14   A shared post that appears on your stream.

After posting your photo, you can click it to use the lightbox view, where you can edit it, add a caption, add tags, and more. See Lesson 8 for more information about working with photos.

Sharing Videos

Sharing videos is another way to enliven your posts. Google+ gives you three ways to share your videos. You can upload from your phone, share from YouTube, or upload from your Android 2.1+ smartphone. Google+ lets you upload an unlimited number of videos of up to 15 minutes each.

To share a video on Google+, follow these steps:

1. Click the **Home** icon at the top of Google+ if you aren't already on your home page (refer to Figure 5.1).

2. Click in the share box to expand it (refer to Figure 5.2).

3. Type your post in the text box. For example, you can introduce or comment on the video you're sharing.

4. Click the **Add Video** button in the lower-right corner of the share box. A pop-up menu opens offering three ways to add videos (see Figure 5.15).

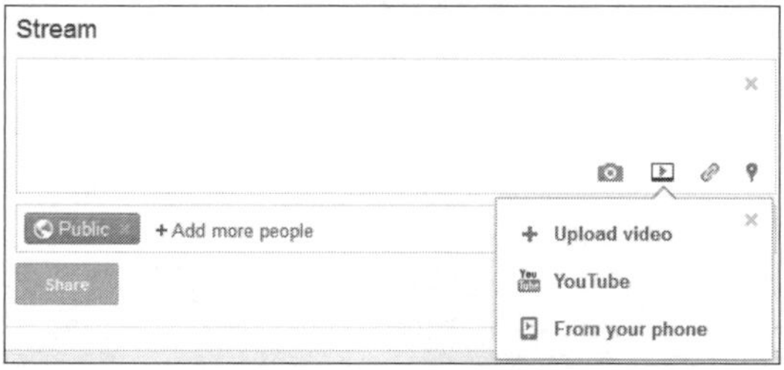

FIGURE 5.15   Google+ gives you three ways to add videos.

5. Attach your video to the post by selecting one of the following menu options:

   ▶ **Upload Video.** Open the **Upload Videos** dialog box, shown in Figure 5.16, from which you can upload videos from your computer. Select the videos you want to upload and click the **Add Videos** button.

   ▶ **YouTube.** Search for YouTube videos by keyword, enter the URL of a specific YouTube video, or select from YouTube videos you've shared in the past. Figure 5.17 shows the **Choose a YouTube Video** dialog box from which you select your video.

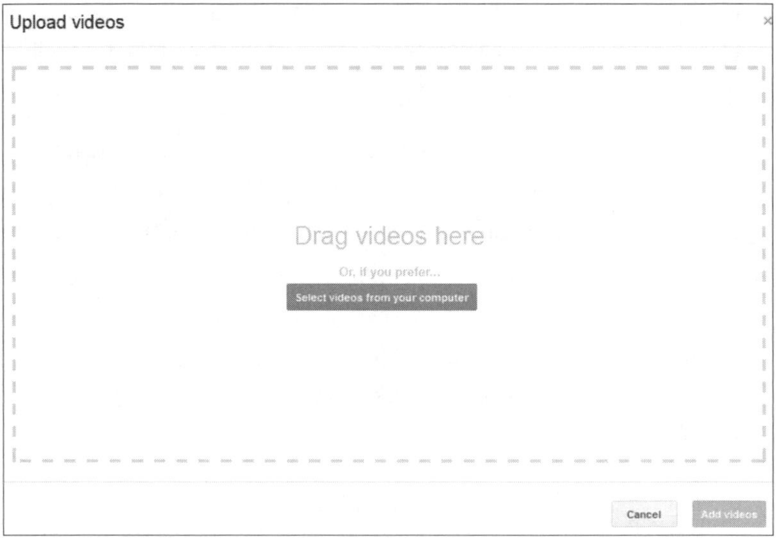

FIGURE 5.16 Add videos from your computer to your Google+ posts.

FIGURE 5.17 Embed a YouTube video on a Google+ post.

▶ **From Your Phone.** Upload videos from your phone. You must have an Android 2.1+ smartphone and download the Google+ for Android app to use this feature. See https://market.android.com/details?id=com.google.android. apps.plus&hl=en for more information about this app.

6. Select the people or circles you want to share this post with or, optionally, make this post public. For a reminder of how to do this, refer to steps 5 through 7 in the section "Using the Share Box" earlier in this lesson.

7. Click the **Share** button to share your post with the people you selected.

Figure 5.18 shows a sample post with a video, which users can click to play.

FIGURE 5.18　　Click this video to play it right on Google+.

Sharing Links

Google+ makes it easy to share links to external websites in your posts. For example, you might want to share your latest blog post or an interesting article you read on the web.

To share a link on Google+, follow these steps:

1. Click the **Home** icon at the top of Google+ if you aren't already on your home page (refer to Figure 5.1).

2. Click in the share box to expand it (refer to Figure 5.2).

3. Type your post in the text box. For example, you can introduce or comment on the link you're sharing.

4. Click the **Add Link** button in the lower-right corner of the share box. The share box expands to display new fields, as shown in Figure 5.19.

FIGURE 5.19   Link to an interesting website or blog post.

5. Enter the complete URL of the website page you want to link to, such as http://www.patricerutledge.com. Optionally, you can copy and paste a longer URL.

6. Click the **Add** button. The share box displays the link name, its description, and an image, as shown in Figure 5.20.

FIGURE 5.20   Preview your link before posting.

> NOTE: **Where Does Google+ Get the Link Data?**
> Google+ retrieves the link name, description, and image from the metadata and content on the site you're linking to. Optionally, you can delete the default description by clicking the **Remove Description** link or delete the default image by clicking the **Delete** button (small x) in the upper-right corner of the image.

7. Select the people or circles you want to share this post with or, optionally, make this post public. For a reminder of how to do this, refer to steps 5 through 7 in the section "Using the Share Box" earlier in this lesson.

8. Click the **Share** button to share your post with the people you selected.

Figure 5.21 shows a sample posted link, visible on the streams of the people you shared with as well as on your public profile if you selected to make this post public.

FIGURE 5.21 Click a link to visit the shared site.

Summary

In this lesson, you learned how to post content on Google+. Next, learn how to view and manage your Google+ stream.

LESSON 6

Viewing Your Google+ Stream

In this lesson, you learn how to view, manage, and participate in your Google+ stream.

Exploring Your Stream

On Google+, the center of activity is your stream. This is the first page you see when you sign into Google+ and the place where you'll spend the majority of your time on the site.

PLAIN ENGLISH: **Google+ Stream**

The Google+ stream offers a central location for viewing the posts, links, photos, and videos that you and others have shared. You can join the conversation on the stream by adding your own posts and comments, sharing interesting content you discover, and supporting quality posts using the Google **+1** button.

Your Google+ stream, shown in Figure 6.1, is divided into three columns:

► The left column enables you to filter your Google+ stream and access chat functionality.

► The center column displays the gravatars of up to 10 people who are in your circles, encourages you to find more people, enables you to post your own content, and displays your posts and the posts submitted by people in your circles.

FIGURE 6.1   Your stream is the center of activity on Google+.

> ▶ The right column displays gravatars (small photos) of people in your circles, suggests more people to add to circles, and enables you to send invitations and start a hangout.

Other lessons in this book cover chat, hangouts, invitations, and sharing content. In this lesson, you'll focus on viewing and managing your Google+ stream.

NOTE: **Why Is My Stream Empty?**

If you're new to Google+ and haven't placed many people in circles yet, your stream could be empty. As soon as you—and the people in your circles—start posting on Google+, you'll see content on your stream.

Accessing Your Stream

Your Google+ stream isn't hard to find. It's the first page you see when you sign into Google+. If you go to another location on Google+, you can return to your stream by clicking the **Home** icon at the top of Google+ (see Figure 6.2).

Home icon

FIGURE 6.2   Click the **Home** icon to view your Google+ stream at any time.

Viewing a Sample Post

Figure 6.3 shows a sample Google+ post shared by someone in one of your circles.

FIGURE 6.3   Viewing a basic post in your Google+ stream.

For each post, you can:

► Pause your mouse over someone's name to view a pop-up with more information about this person.

► Click someone's name to view this person's Google+ profile.

► Click the date to view other posts from that date.

► Click the **Limited** link to view gravatars of people the post author shared with. The **Limited** link displays only when the author shared this content with specific circles rather than publicly. If the **Public** link displays instead, the author shared the content publicly and it's visible to anyone on the web.

► Click the **+1** button to show your support for this post using Google +1. See "Liking a Post Using the +1 Button," later in this lesson for more information.

► Click the **Comment** link to add a comment. See "Commenting on Posts" later in this lesson for more information.

▶ Click the **Share** link to share this post with others. See "Sharing Posts" later in this lesson for more information.

Depending on the actions of the original author and the people reading the post, other content might be available. Figure 6.4 shows a post with additional content and conversation.

FIGURE 6.4   Viewing a post with lots of conversation.

When a post contains additional content or activity, other options for interaction become available. For example, you can:

▶ Click a link to view content from an external site, such as a blog post that someone shared on Google+.

▶ Click an attached photo to enlarge it or add tags to it. See Lesson 8, "Working with Photos," for more information about tagging photos.

▶ Click a video to play it in Google+.

▶ Pause your mouse over the name of someone mentioned in a post to view a pop-up box with more information about this person.

Optionally, click the person's name to view this person's profile. Google+ identifies a mention by placing the plus sign (+) before someone's name, such as +Anne Smith.

▶ View the number of +1's. Click the **+[number]** link to view a complete list of people who shared. For example, if 8 people shared this post, the link name would be +8.

▶ View the number of shares, including the names of some people who shared this post. Click the **[Number] Shares** link to view a complete list of people who shared. For example, if 12 people shared this post, the link name would be 12 Shares.

▶ View the most recent comments at the end of a post. To view additional comments, click the **[Number] Comments** link. Click the **Expand This Comment** link to view the entire text of longer comments. You can also add your own comment to an existing comment. See "Commenting on Posts" later in this lesson for more information.

Be aware that all of these options might not be available for every post. For example, not all posts contain links, videos, photos, mentions, comments, shares, and +1's.

Filtering Your Stream

By default, Google+ displays both your posts and the posts of people in your circles on your stream. If you have a large network with many circles, however, your stream can become overloaded with too much content.

To filter your stream, click the name of a circle in the **Streams** section on the left side of the page (see Figure 6.5).

Google+ displays only the posts from the people in this circle. For example, if you click the **Friends** link, your stream displays only posts from people in this circle.

If you want to view only your own posts, click the **Profile** icon at the top of Google+. All your posts display on the **Posts** tab of your profile.

FIGURE 6.5   You can filter your stream by circle.

NOTE: **Why Did My Content Disappear When I Applied a Filter?**

Be aware that if no one in a circle has posted on Google+, you won't see any content when you filter to that circle. This is particularly common if you have only a few people in a circle and they are new to Google+.

TIP: **Google+ Displays Game-Related Posts on the Games Stream**

If you enjoy playing games, Google+ displays all posts related to your gaming activities on the Games stream and not on the main Google+ stream. This way, only your game buddies need to know about your high score on Bejeweled Blitz or your other game achievements. See Lesson 11, "Playing Games," for more information about Google+ games and the Games stream.

Viewing Your Incoming Stream

Your Incoming stream displays content shared by people who have you in their circles but aren't in one of your circles. Figure 6.6 shows this stream.

For example, if your colleague Dalton adds you to his Acquaintances circle, but you don't add him to any of your circles, Dalton's posts display only on the Incoming stream.

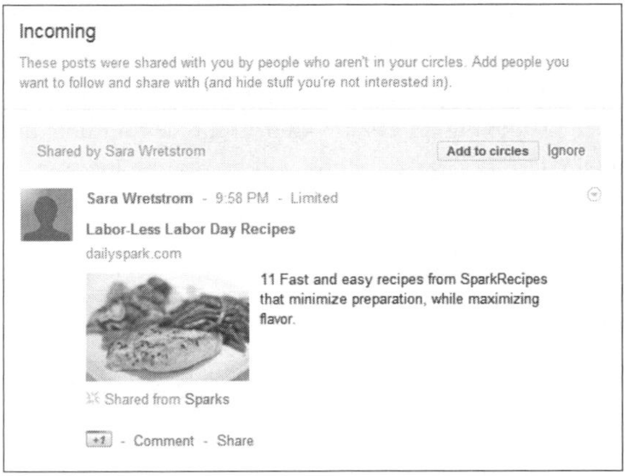

FIGURE 6.6 The Incoming stream displays posts from people you don't follow but follow you.

The Incoming stream is similar to your regular stream but includes two additional options. On the Incoming stream, you can:

▶ **Add someone to one of your circles.** Pause your mouse over the **Add to Circles** button next to the name of a person you want to add to a circle. Google+ opens a pop-up box that lists your available circles (see Figure 6.7). Select the checkbox to the left of the circle to which you want to add this person. See Lesson 3, "Managing Your Network with Circles," for more information.

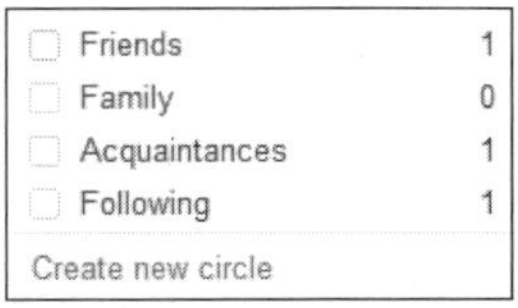

FIGURE 6.7 If you find someone interesting on your Incoming stream, you can add this person to one of your circles.

▶ **Hide someone's posts.** Click the **Ignore** link (refer to Figure 6.6) to hide this person's posts from your Incoming stream. For example, you might want to ignore someone who posts content you aren't interested in or posts in a language you don't know. If you make a mistake, you can undo this action, as shown in Figure 6.8. You can also take stronger action and block this person as well. See "Blocking a Person" later in this lesson for more information about blocking someone and its ramifications.

FIGURE 6.8   Google+ confirms that you no longer want to see posts from this person.

You can also link to a post, report abuse, mute a post, or block a person on the Incoming stream, just as you can on your main stream. See "Managing Your Circles' Posts in the Stream" later in this lesson for more information.

Viewing Notifications

The **Notifications** page alerts you to Google+ activity that relates to you or your content. To view the **Notifications** page, click the **Home** icon at the top of Google+ and click the **Notifications** link on the left side of the page. Figure 6.9 shows the **Notifications** page.

FIGURE 6.9   View all of your Google+ notifications in one place.

Understanding How Notifications Work

The **Notifications** page alerts you when someone:

▶ Adds you to a circle

▶ Mentions your name in a post

▶ Comments on one of your posts

▶ Comments on a post you commented on

▶ +1's one of your posts

▶ Tags you in a photo

▶ Comments on one of your photos

▶ Shares a post with you

▶ Invites you to Google+ or accepts your Google+ invitation

TIP: **Receive Notifications on the Google+ Bar, by Email, or by Text Message**

Google+ also alerts you to your notifications through the **Notifications** button on the Google+ bar, which highlights your number of new notifications in red. Another option is to receive notifications by email or text message for specific Google+ actions. See Lesson 7, "Using the Google+ Bar," and Lesson 4, "Managing Google+ Settings and Privacy," for more information.

Filtering the Notifications Page

To filter your notifications on the **Notifications** page, click the **More** link in the upper-right corner of this page and select one of the following options (see Figure 6.10):

▶ Added to Circles

▶ Posts by You

▶ Posts by Others

▶ Mentions

▶ Photo Tags

▶ Games

Google+ filters the **Notifications** page to display only the selected notifications.

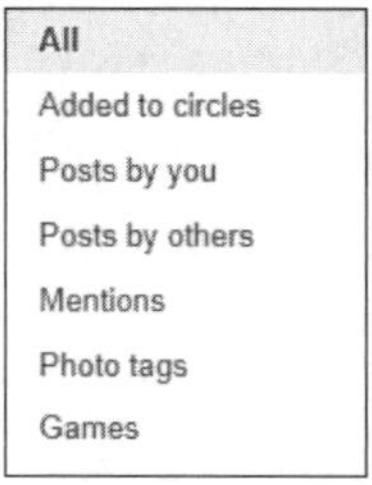

All
Added to circles
Posts by you
Posts by others
Mentions
Photo tags
Games

FIGURE 6.10   Filter your content by notification type.

Participating in the Stream

After you've spent some time reading posts in your stream, you'll probably want to join the conversation and start adding your own commentary. Google+ gives you the option to show your support for a post with +1, add a comment to a post, or share a post.

Liking a Post Using the +1 Button

One of the fastest and easiest ways to let people know that you like specific content in your Google+ stream is to use the +1 button.

PLAIN ENGLISH: **Google +1 Button**

The Google **+1 button** offers a way to publicly show your support for a post that you like. The +1 button is available on Google+ and, optionally, on other websites and blogs that choose to enable this button. Google+ uses the term "+1" as both a noun and verb. In other words, you +1 a post using the +1 button. To learn more about the concept behind the Google +1 button, visit www.google.com/+1/button.

If you want to show others that you like a post in your stream, click the **+1** button that displays below the post content (see Figure 6.11).

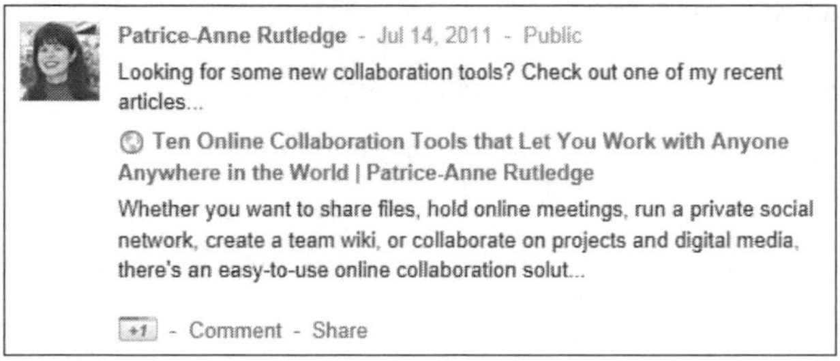

FIGURE 6.11   Click the +1 button to show your support for a post.

Your stream shows that you +1'd the post (see Figure 6.12). Be aware that this action is public and others can also see that you +1'd the post.

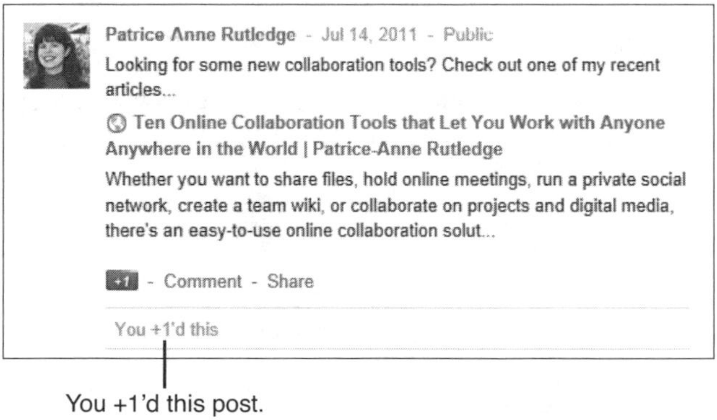

You +1'd this post.

FIGURE 6.12   You can see the posts you +1'd in your stream.

TIP: **Show Your Support for a Comment Using the +1 Button**

Using the **+1** button isn't reserved for posts; you can use it to support comments as well. If you want to show your support for a particularly interesting or insightful comment, click the **+1** button directly below it.

Commenting on Posts

If you have something to say about a post, you can add your own commentary.

To add a comment, follow these steps:

1. Click the **Comment** link at the bottom of the post you want to comment on.

2. Type your comment in the text box that displays (see Figure 6.13).

FIGURE 6.13   Join the conversation on Google+ by adding your own comments.

3. Click the **Post Comment** button to post your comment. Figure 6.14 shows a sample published comment.

FIGURE 6.14   Your comment displays at the end of a post.

TIP: **Apply Styles and Mention People in a Comment**

Just like with a post, you can apply styles such as bolding and italics to your comment text. You can also mention other Google+ users and include a link to their profile. See Lesson 5, "Sharing Content on Google+," for more information about applying styles and mentioning other Google+ users.

Editing a Comment

After posting a comment, you might notice a typo or think of something else you want to add.

To edit a comment you wrote, follow these steps:

1. Click the **Edit** link below the comment.

2. Make your changes in the text box, as shown in Figure 6.15.

FIGURE 6.15   If you make a mistake, you can edit a comment.

3. Click the **Save Changes** button.

Google+ updates your comment with the changes you made.

Deleting a Comment

If you decide that posting your comment wasn't such a good idea after all, you can delete it.

To delete a comment you wrote, click the **Edit** link below the comment and then click the **Delete Comment** button (see Figure 6.16).

FIGURE 6.16   Delete your comment if you no longer want to display it.

Google+ permanently deletes your comment.

Sharing Posts

When you find an interesting post on Google+, you can share it with others. You can also share post comments.

To share a post, follow these steps:

1. Click the **Share** link below the post you want to share, as shown in Figure 6.17.

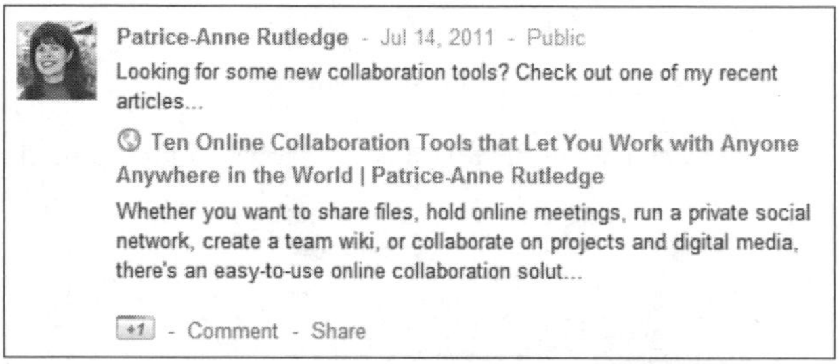

FIGURE 6.17   Share interesting posts with others on Google+.

CAUTION: **Consider Carefully Who You Share With**

If the original author shared this post only with a limited audience (such as people in circles), Google+ reminds you of this fact and encourages you to use discretion when sharing. In general, it's good etiquette to focus on sharing posts that others made public rather than only with those in their chosen circles.

2. In the **Share This Post** box, add your own comments about the post in the text box. Figure 6.18 shows the **Share This Post** box.

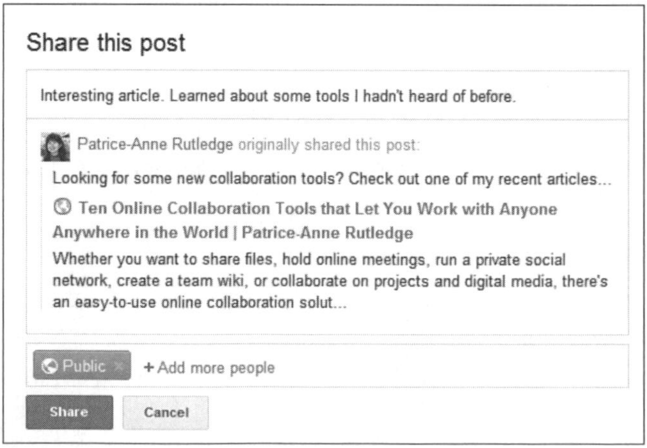

FIGURE 6.18   Add your own comments to the content you share.

3. If the original author made this post public, Google+ makes your shared version public as well, visible to anyone on the web. If you don't want to share this post publicly, click the **Delete** icon (x) on the right side of the **Public** button. If the original author shared this post only with a limited audience, you can share it with your circles but not publicly.

4. To share this post with specific circles, click the **Add More People** link.

5. In the menu that opens (see Figure 6.19), select the circles you want to share with. If you want to share with all your circles, select **Your Circles.** If you want to share with your extended circles (friends of friends), select **Extended Circles.**

Friends (1)

Family (0)

Acquaintances (1)

Following (1)

Your circles

Extended circles

FIGURE 6.19 You can choose the specific circles you want to share with.

6. When you're finished selecting circles, click outside the menu to close it.

7. If you want to send a notification and email about this post to the people in a circle, hover the mouse above that circle and select the **Notify About This Post** checkbox. In general, you should send notifications and emails only for very urgent or important posts.

8. If any of the people in your selected circles aren't on Google+ yet, you have the option to send them an email about this post. To do so, click the **Also Email [Number of] People Not Yet Using Google+** checkbox. To view the people who will receive this email click the **[Number of] People** link. For example, if

two people you added to circles haven't signed up for Google+
yet, this link says "2 People." Again, use caution when emailing
people and send emails only for very important content.

9. Click the **Share** button to share your post with the people you
   selected.

Figure 6.20 shows a sample shared post, visible on the streams of the people you shared with as well as on your public profile if you selected to
make this post public. Your Google+ network can comment on, share, or
+1 any post you share.

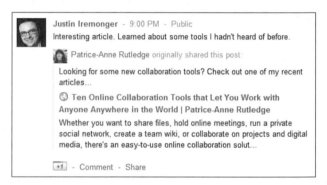

FIGURE 6.20   A shared post that appears on your stream.

Managing Your Posts in the Stream

After you share posts to the Google+ stream, you might want to make a
few changes. To manage a post you created, click the small down arrow in
the upper-right corner of the post to open the **Options** menu. By selecting
an option from this menu, you can edit a post, delete a post, report or
remove comments, disable comments, or lock a post. This menu displays
only for your own posts. See "Managing Your Circles' Posts in the
Stream" later in this lesson to learn about the menu options available for
posts from people in your circles.

> TIP: **View All Your Posts on Your Profile**
>
> If you want to view only your own posts rather than the mixed assortment of posts that display on your stream, you can do so on the **Posts** tab of your profile. The **Options** menu is available there as well.

Editing a Post

For example, you can edit a post to fix a typo; to add a photo, video, or link you forgot to include; or delete something you regret posting.

To edit one of your posts, follow these steps:

1. Click the down arrow in the upper-right corner of your post to open the Options menu, as shown in Figure 6.21.

FIGURE 6.21   If you make a mistake, you can edit your post.

2. Select **Edit This Post** from the **Options** menu. Google+ opens the post in Edit mode, as shown in Figure 6.22.

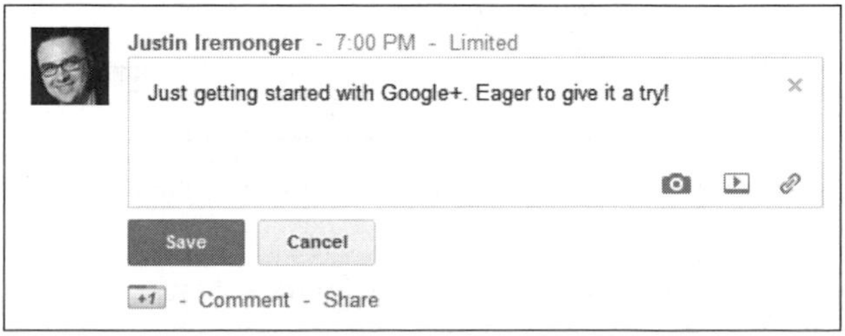

FIGURE 6.22   Edit your content in the text box.

3. Make your changes in the text box. If you're editing content you posted yourself, the **Add Photos**, **Add Video**, and **Add Link** buttons display in the lower-right corner, giving you the opportunity to add content to your post. If you're editing a post you shared, these buttons aren't available. See Lesson 5 for more information about sharing photos, videos, or links.

4. Click the **Save** button to save your changes and update your post.

CAUTION: **Post Edits Don't Transfer to Shared Content**

If someone shared your post before you edited it, the original version of the post will remain in any shared locations. If a post contains a serious error that needs to be changed, you must ask the people who shared to delete and share again.

Deleting a Post

To delete one of your posts, follow these steps:

1. Click the down arrow in the upper-right corner of your post.

2. Select **Delete This Post** from the **Options** menu (refer to Figure 6.21).

3. Click the **Delete** button in the dialog box that opens to confirm the deletion (see Figure 6.23). Google+ permanently removes the post from your stream. You can no longer view this post nor can anyone you shared it with.

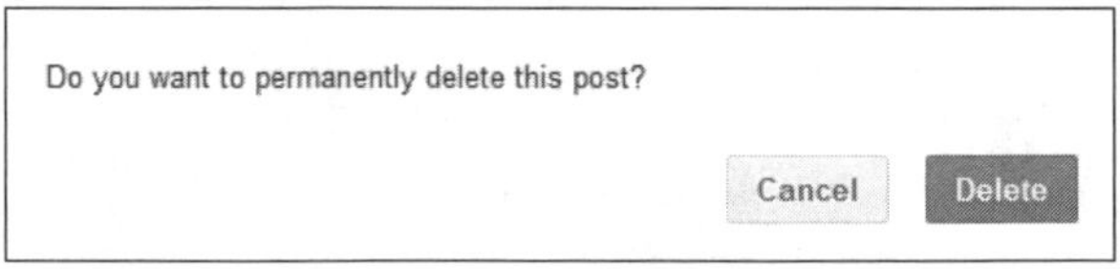

Do you want to permanently delete this post?

Cancel   Delete

FIGURE 6.23   Confirm that you really want to delete your post.

CAUTION: **Deleting Doesn't Remove Shared Posts**

If someone shared your post before you deleted it, the shared version of the post will remain on Google+. To delete the shared versions of your posts, you must ask the people who shared to

> delete as well. If you don't want people to be able to share a post, you should lock it. See "Locking a Post" later in this lesson for more information.

Disabling Comments

If you don't want people to comment on a post, you can disable comments for it.

To disable comments for a post, click the down arrow in the upper-right corner of the post and select **Disable Comments** from the **Options** menu (refer to Figure 6.21).

Google+ removes the **Comments** link at the bottom of the post but retains any existing comments. Optionally, you can also remove any existing comments. See "Reporting or Removing Comments" later in this lesson for more information.

If you want to enable comments again, click the down arrow in the upper-right corner of the post and select **Enable Comments** from the Options menu.

Reporting or Removing Comments

If others have commented on your post, you can report or remove any comment.

Reporting a Comment

If someone posts an inappropriate comment in response to one of your posts, you can report it to Google.

> CAUTION: **Consider Carefully Which Comments to Report as Abuse**
>
> You can report comments that violate Google+ terms and conditions (spam, nudity, hate speech, violence, copyright abuse, or child abuse). If someone simply disagrees with your post, you can remove the comment. Comments with dissenting opinions don't constitute abuse unless someone repeatedly posts comments to the point of harassment.

To report a comment, follow these steps:

1. Click the down arrow in the upper-right corner of the post.

2. Select **Report or Remove Comments** from the **Options** menu (refer to Figure 6.21).

3. Click the **Report Abuse** button (a small flag icon) to the right of the comment you want to report, as shown in Figure 6.24.

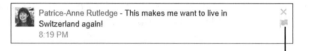

Report Abuse button

FIGURE 6.24   Click the flag icon to report abuse.

Google+ reviews all reports of abuse and takes appropriate action if necessary.

Removing a Comment

If you find an inappropriate or annoying comment on one of your posts, you can remove it.

To remove a comment, follow these steps:

1. Click the down arrow in the upper-right corner of the post.

2. Select **Report or Remove Comments** from the **Options** menu (refer to Figure 6.21).

3. Click the **Remove** button (x) to the right of the comment you want to remove (refer to Figure 6.24). Google+ removes the comment from your post.

Locking a Post

If you want to prevent others from sharing a post, you can lock it.

To lock a post, click the down arrow in the upper-right corner of your post and select **Lock This Post** from the **Options** menu (refer to Figure 6.21).

Google+ alerts you that people can no longer share this post and removes the Share link at the bottom of the post.

If you want to unlock a post, click the down arrow in the upper-right corner of the post and select **Unlock This Post** from the **Options** menu.

Managing Your Circles' Posts in the Stream

Google+ also enables you to manage the content the people in your circles post. To manage a post of someone in one of your circles, click the small down arrow in the upper-right corner of the post to open the **Options** menu. By selecting an option from this menu, you can link to a post, report abuse, mute a post, or block the person who posted. This menu displays only for posts the people in your circles create. See "Managing Your Posts in the Stream" earlier in this lesson to learn about the menu options available for posts you create.

Linking to a Post

You can link to a specific Google+ post from an external website or blog.

To link to a Google+ post, follow these steps:

1. Click the down arrow in the upper-right corner of your post (see Figure 6.25).

FIGURE 6.25   Select Link to This Post from the Options menu that opens.

2. Select **Link to This Post** from the **Options** menu. Google+ opens the post in a new window (see Figure 6.26).

3. Copy and paste the URL on the site you want to include the link.

Post URL

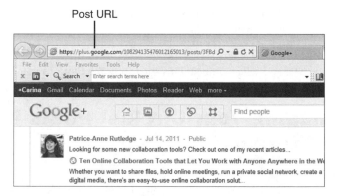

FIGURE 6.26   Copy the URL to link to it from your website or blog.

Reporting Abuse

If someone posts content that violates Google's terms and conditions, you can report it.

To report abuse, follow these steps:

1. Click the down arrow in the upper-right corner of the post.

2. Select **Report Abuse** from the **Options** menu (refer to Figure 6.25).

3. In the **Report This Post** dialog box, shown in Figure 6.27, select the reason for reporting abuse: spam, nudity, hate speech or violence, child abuse, copyright, or for another reason (such as someone impersonating you or a public figure).

4. Click the **Submit** button to submit your report to Google. Google reviews all reports of abuse and takes any necessary action.

CAUTION: **Consider Carefully When to Report Content as Abuse**

You can report content that violates Google+ terms and conditions (spam, nudity, hate speech, violence, copyright, or child abuse). If someone invites you to a game you don't want to play, you should just hide the notification. Game invitations don't constitute abuse unless someone repeatedly sends you invitations to the point of harassment.

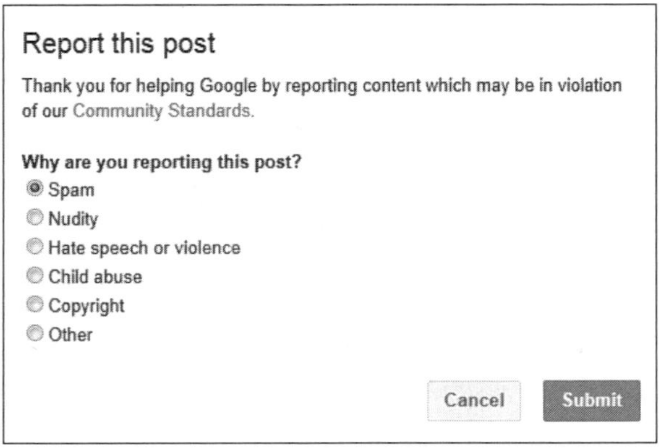

FIGURE 6.27   Let Google know why this post is abusive.

If this post has comments, you must click the flag icon next to the specific content you want to report (the post itself or one of the comments).

Muting a Post

When you comment on a post, you receive a notification any time someone else comments on that same post. Although you might want to read what your friends have to say about a pertinent topic, you might rather not receive a large volume of notifications about people you don't know. This is particularly common if you comment on a post that generates a lot of response from the Google+ community. To avoid this problem, you can mute the post. Muting removes a post from your stream and stops sending you notifications about future comments.

To mute a post, click the down arrow in the upper-right corner of the post and select **Mute This Post** from the **Options** menu (refer to Figure 6.25).

Google+ lets you know that the post is muted, as shown in Figure 6.28. To view the post again, click the **Undo Mute** link.

Blocking a Person

If you no longer want to interact with someone on Google+, you can block this person.

FIGURE 6.28   Mute posts that become overwhelmed with irrelevant chatter.

When you block people, Google+ removes them from your circles and extended circles, and their posts no longer display on your main or Incoming stream. In addition, they can't comment on your content posted after you blocked them or mention you in their posts or comments.

Be aware, however, that blocked people can still view your public content on Google+ and can place you in their own circles.

To block someone, follow these steps:

1. Click the down arrow in the upper-right corner of the post.

2. Select **Block This Person** from the **Options** menu (refer to Figure 6.25).

3. Confirm that you want to block this person.

You can also block people on the Incoming stream or on their profile.

CAUTION: **Consider Other Options Before Blocking Someone**

Blocking is a strong action which should be reserved for those people who are posting inappropriate content or are harassing you on Google+. You should consider other options before choosing to block someone. For example, you can remove people from your circles if you don't want to share with them anymore. You can ignore people whose posts you don't want to see on your Incoming stream. Or, if you just don't want to see a post anymore, you can hide it.

Searching for Posts in Your Stream

If you can't find a specific post in your stream or are looking for posts on a specific topic, Google+ search can help.

To search your stream, follow these steps:

1. Enter your search term in the search box at the top of Google+.

2. Click the **Google+ Posts** link to view posts that match this search term, as shown in Figure 6.29.

FIGURE 6.29   Quickly find Google+ posts from your stream on any topic.

3. By default, Google+ displays its opinion of the best posts on this topic. Optionally, click the **Most Recent** link to display posts in chronological order.

4. If you want to save this search for future use, click the **Save This Search** button in the upper-right corner of the page. Google+ displays this term on the left side of your home page, where you can click it at any time to view posts on this topic.

Optionally, you can click the following links on the Google+ search page for additional search results:

- ▶ **Everything.** Display Google+ posts, people, and web content related to this search term.

- ▶ **People.** Display people related to this search term. Click the **Add to Circles** button next to someone's name to add this person to one of your circles.

- ▶ **Sparks.** Display popular content from around the web related to this search term.

Summary

In this lesson, you learned how to manage your Google+ stream. Next, learn how the Google+ bar makes it easier to get things done on Google+.

LESSON 7

Using the Google+ Bar

In this lesson, you learn how to use the Google+ bar to access popular Google+ features.

Exploring the Google+ Bar

The Google+ bar is a handy toolbar that displays at the top of any Google product, including Google+, Google (the search engine), Gmail, Google Reader, and so forth.

If you aren't signed in to Google+, the bar offers the basic features shown in Figure 7.1.

Web Images Videos Maps News Shopping Gmail more ▾   Sign in ⚙

FIGURE 7.1   The Google+ bar offers limited tools if you're not signed in to Google+.

After signing in to Google+, additional features are available on the Google+ bar (see Figure 7.2).

FIGURE 7.2   Access popular Google+ features on the Google+ bar.

From left to right, the tools available on the Google+ Bar are:

> ▶ **+[First Name].** Open your Google+ profile. For example, if your first name is Anne, this link displays as "+Anne".

- ▶ **Links to access Gmail, Calendar, Documents, Photos, Reader, and the Web (this takes you to www.google.com).** Click the **More** link to display a drop-down list of other products, including YouTube, News, Maps, Books, and more.

- ▶ **[Full Name].** Open a menu of popular Google+ features. For example, if your name is Anne Smith, this link displays as "Anne Smith."

- ▶ **Notifications button.** View notifications of recent Google+ activity, such as people who have added you to their circles.

- ▶ **Share button.** Share content on Google+.

- ▶ **Your gravatar (a small photo).** Open a menu of popular Google+ features.

- ▶ **Options button.** Open a menu with options to access Google+ settings, Google+ Help, and your web history. You can also send feedback to Google+ from this menu.

Viewing Your Notifications

Notifications alert you to important activities on Google+. You receive a notification whenever someone:

- ▶ Invites you to Google+

- ▶ Adds you to one of their Google+ circles

- ▶ Tags you in a photo

- ▶ Shares a post with you directly

- ▶ Adds a comment to one of your posts

The **Notifications** button on the Google+ bar tells you how many unread notifications you have by highlighting this number in red. In Figure 7.3, for example, you have two unread notifications.

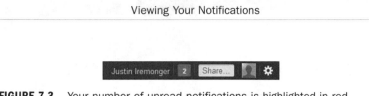

FIGURE 7.3 Your number of unread notifications is highlighted in red.

> NOTE: **Why Is the Notifications Button Blank?**
>
> If you don't have any unread notifications, numbers don't display on the Notifications button, and the button isn't highlighted in red. You can still click the Notifications button to view previously read notifications.

To view and react to your notifications, follow these steps:

1. Click the **Notifications** button in the upper-right corner of the Google+ bar (refer to Figure 7.2). Figure 7.4 shows some sample notifications. Google+ groups your notifications by type, such as notifications that let you know someone added you to a circle.

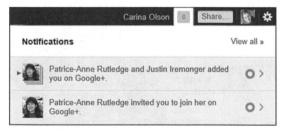

FIGURE 7.4 View your notifications by type.

2. Click the arrow to the right of a notification to view its detail menu, as shown in Figure 7.5. For example, you can view all the people who recently added you to a circle.

3. Take any of the following actions:

   ▶ Click someone's name to open that person's profile.

   ▶ Pause your mouse over someone's name to view a pop-up box with more information including a headline and the people you share in common, as shown in Figure 7.6.

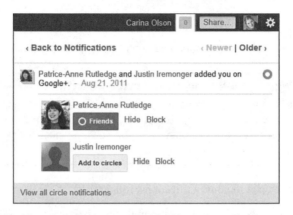

FIGURE 7.5   View the people associated with each notification type.

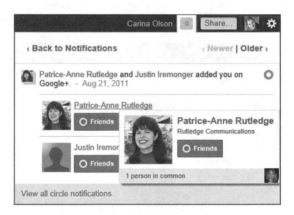

FIGURE 7.6   View more information about someone in the pop-up box.

▶ Pause your mouse over the **Add to Circles** button below the name of a person you want to add to a circle. In the pop-up box that opens (see Figure 7.7), select the checkbox next to the circle to which you want to add this person. Optionally, click the **Create New Circle** link to add this person to a new circle. If you've already added someone to a circle, the **Add to Circles** button is replaced with a button that displays the name of the circle this person belongs to.

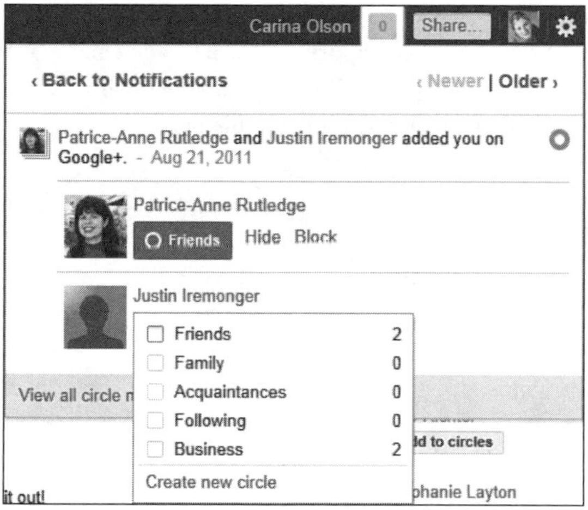

FIGURE 7.7   Quickly add people to circles.

▶ Click the **Hide** link to hide someone from the Notifications menu. For example, you can hide someone you don't know and don't plan to add to one of your circles. However, if you later change your mind, click **Undo**, and they will no longer be hidden.

▶ Click the **Block** link to block someone from Google+. Blocking is a stronger action than hiding. When you block people on Google+, they will no longer be in any of your circles, their posts no longer display on your Incoming stream, and they can't comment on your posts. The people you block are not aware that you have blocked them. See Lesson 6, "Viewing Your Google+ Stream," for more information about the ramifications of blocking people.

From the Notifications detail menu, you can also do the following:

▶ Click the **Back to Notifications** link to return to the initial Notifications menu.

▶ Click the **Older** link or **Newer** link to move to older or newer notifications.

▶ Click the **View All Circle Notifications** link to open the Notifications page (see Figure 7.8) where you can view all your notifications in one place. Clicking the **View All** link on the initial Notifications menu also opens this page.

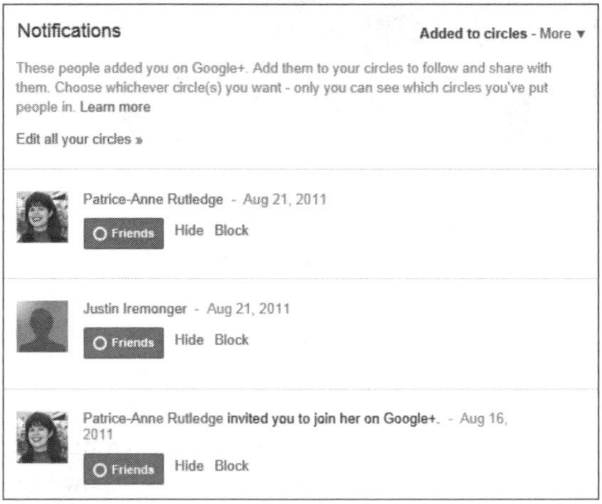

FIGURE 7.8   View all your notifications on one page.

To close the Notifications menu, click another part of the Google+ screen.

Accessing Popular Google+ Features

The Google+ bar gives you quick access to popular Google+ features. When you click your full name or your gravatar (small photo) on the right side of the Google+ bar, a pop-up box opens. Figure 7.9 shows this pop-up box.

In this box, you can click the following links:

▶ **Profile.** Open your Google+ profile, described in Lesson 2, "Working with Google+ Profiles."

FIGURE 7.9   Quickly access popular features.

▶ **Circles.** Open the **Circles** page, described in Lesson 3,
  "Managing Your Network with Circles."

▶ **Account Settings.** Open the **Account Overview** page, described
  in Lesson 4, "Managing Google+ Settings and Privacy."

▶ **Privacy.** Open the **Profile and Privacy** page, described in
  Lesson 4.

▶ **Switch Account.** Open a new menu that enables you to sign in to
  another account or sign out of all accounts. You must enable
  multiple sign-ins accounts at https://www.google.com/accounts/
  MultipleSessions to view this link. See Lesson 4 for more information about multiple sign-ins.

▶ **Sign Out.** Sign out of Google+.

Sharing Content

You can share content directly from the Google+ bar. To do so, click the
Share button on the bar to open a pop-up box (see Figure 7.10) with fields
similar to those on your home page share box.

See Lesson 5, "Sharing Content on Google+," to learn more about sharing
your content.

FIGURE 7.10   The Google+ bar offers another way to share content.

Getting Help

Although *Sams Teach Yourself Google+ in 10 Minutes* should provide answers to most of your Google+ questions, there are times when you might want to refer to online help. For example, Google+ Help keeps you updated on new Google+ features that are released after this book's publication.

To access Google+ online help, click the **Options** button located on the far right side of the Google+ bar and select Google+ Help from the drop-down menu. The Google+ Help page opens, shown in Figure 7.11.

Here you can search for answers to your questions, review information about popular topics, and learn what's new on Google+.

Sending Feedback

If you run into a problem on Google+ or want to give Google suggestions about future features or improvements, you can submit feedback.

To submit feedback to Google, follow these steps:

1. Click the **Options** button on the Google+ bar (refer to Figure 7.2). Click **Send Feedback** and the **Send Feedback** dialog box opens, shown in Figure 7.12. Depending on your operating system and browser, the appearance of this dialog box could vary.

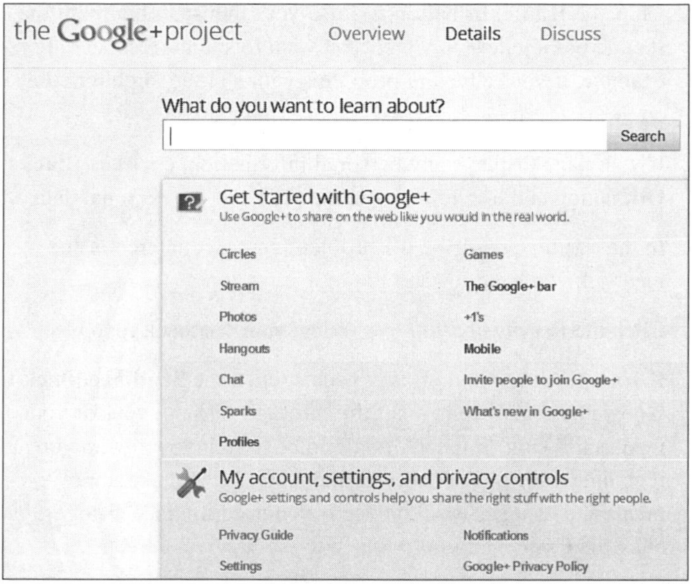

FIGURE 7.11   Learn what's new on Google+.

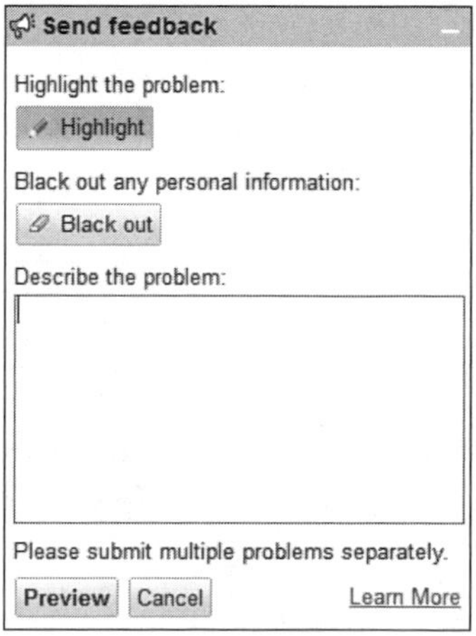

FIGURE 7.12   Send Google your feedback about Google+.

2. Click the **Highlight** button and use your mouse to highlight the section of Google+ on which you want to submit feedback. For example, if you're having problems with a circle, highlight that circle.

3. If your page displays any personal information, click the **Black Out** button and use your mouse to black out the personal data.

4. In the text box, describe the problem you encountered or the feedback you want to send to Google.

5. Click the **Preview** button to preview your feedback report.

6. If your preview displays as expected, click the **Send Feedback to Google** button. You then get the message, "Thank you for your feedback!" Don't expect Google to be back in touch with you regarding your issue. They use the feedback to make improvements and changes to Google+. If you need to make changes, click the **Cancel** button to return to the previous screen.

Optionally, you can also click the **Send Feedback** button in the lower-right corner of any Google+ page to open the **Send Feedback** dialog box.

TIP: **Submit One Feedback Report per Problem**

If you have multiple problems, submit a feedback report for each problem. This makes it easier for Google to categorize and respond to your feedback.

Signing Out

If you're using a public computer or other people have ready access to your own computer, you should sign out of Google+ when you're finished using it.

To do so, click either your full name or your gravatar on the right side of the Google+ bar and then click the **Sign Out** link in the pop-up box that opens (refer to Figure 7.9).

Summary

In this lesson, you learned how to use the Google+ bar for handy access to popular Google+ features. Now it's time to learn more about the many photo options Google+ provides.

LESSON 8

Working with Photos

In this lesson, you learn how to upload, edit, and manage photos.

Exploring Google+ Photo Options

Google+ offers a comprehensive photo management solution, enabling you to upload, store, and share unlimited photos. You can upload photos up to 2,048 x 2,048 pixels in size. Google+ resizes photos larger than this.

Your photos display on the stream as well as on the **Photos** tab of your profile. Optionally, you can hide this tab. You also maintain complete control over who can view your photos. For example, you can share photos on the stream publicly, or share only with people in specific circles or your extended circle.

> NOTE: **Google+ Integrates with Picasa Web Albums**
>
> Google+ integrates directly with Picasa Web Albums, Google's digital photo-management web application. To go to Picasa Web Albums, click the **Photos** link on the Google+ bar. When you upload photos to Google+, they are automatically available on Picasa Web Albums as well. As with Google+, you have complete control over who can view your web albums.

Uploading Photos to Google+

Google+ provides several places to upload and share photos:

- ▶ **From the share box.** You can access this box on your stream or by clicking the **Share** button on the Google+ bar. Click the **Add Photos** icon in the lower-right corner of the share box to upload photos from your computer, create a photo album, or upload photos from your Android 2.1+ smartphone. See Lesson 5, "Sharing Content on Google+," for more information.

▶ **From the Google+ Photos page.** Click the **Upload New Photos** button to create a photo album. This button is available on the **Photos from Your Circles** and **Your Albums** tabs. See "Creating and Managing Photo Albums" later in this lesson for more information.

▶ **From the Photos tab on your profile.** Click the **Upload Photos** button to create a photo album. See "Creating and Managing Photo Albums" later in this lesson for more information.

Exploring the Photos Page

The **Photos** page offers a centralized location to manage your photos and photo albums on Google+. To access the **Photos** page, click the **Photos** icon at the top of Google+, as shown in Figure 8.1.

Photos icon

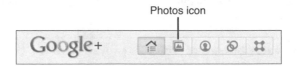

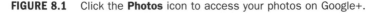

FIGURE 8.1   Click the **Photos** icon to access your photos on Google+.

The Photos page has four tabs:

▶ **Photos from Your Circle.** View photos from people in your circles (see Figure 8.2). If a photo has comments, the number of comments displays in the **Comments** icon in the upper-right corner of the photo. Click a photo to open it in lightbox view. See "Working the the Photo Lightbox" later in this lesson for more information.

▶ **Photos from Your Phone.** View and manage photos you uploaded from your phone. You must have an Android 2.1+ smartphone and download the Google+ for Android app to use this feature. Google+ uploads the photos you take from your phone and places them on this tab, where they remain private

FIGURE 8.2 View photos posted by people in your circles.

until you choose to share them. See https://market.android.com/
details?id=com.google.android.apps.plus for more information
about this app.

▶ **Photos of You.** View photos tagged with your name (see Figure
8.3). Note that even if you upload a profile photo of yourself, you
need to tag it with your name for it to display on this tab. See
"Tagging Photos" later in this lesson for more information.

FIGURE 8.3 View photos tagged with your name.

▶ **Your albums.** Add, view, and manage photo albums. See
"Creating and Managing Photo Albums" for more information.

Creating and Managing Photo Albums

A photo album is a collection of photos, usually on a specific topic or
taken at a specific place or event. You can post and share photo albums on
Google+ just like you do individual photos.

TIP: **Use a Photo Album to Post a Slide Deck on Google+**

You can also use a photo album to post a slide deck on Google+. For example, export all the slides in a PowerPoint presentation to images and post them as an album. Your Google+ network can comment on each slide/photo individually or the presentation as a whole.

Google+ enables you to create a photo album from the share box on your stream and Google+ bar, the **Photos** page, or the **Photos** tab on your profile. The process is similar for all three.

Creating a Photo Album

To create a photo album from the **Photos** page, follow these steps:

1. Click the **Photos** icon at the top of Google+ (refer to Figure 8.1).

2. Click the **Upload New Photos** button in the upper-right corner of the page.

3. In the **Upload and Share Photos** dialog box, shown in Figure 8.4, enter a name for your photo album in the **Album Name** field. By default, Google+ displays the current date as your album name, but changing this to a more meaningful name makes it easier to identify your photo albums.

4. Click the **Select Photos from Your Computer** button.

TIP: **Add Multiple Photos Quickly Using Drag and Drop**

If you want to upload multiple photos to your photo album, you can drag them to the **Upload and Share Photos** dialog box. For example, if you have Windows Explorer open in a separate, minimized window, you can select multiple files and drag them to this dialog box all at once.

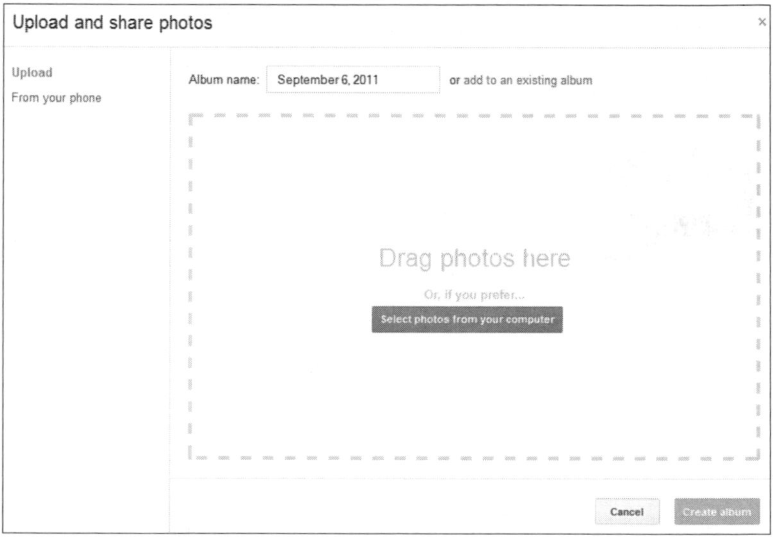

FIGURE 8.4   Give your album a descriptive, meaningful name.

5. In the **Choose File to Upload** dialog box, select the first photo
   you want to add and click the **Open** button. Depending on your
   operating system and browser, this dialog box and button might
   have different names.

6. This photo displays in the **Upload and Share Photos** dialog box,
   shown in Figure 8.5. Optionally, click the photo to rotate it left or
   right, or delete it. You can also edit photos using the lightbox. See
   "Working in the Photo Lightbox" later in this lesson for more
   information.

7. Click the **Upload More** link to continue uploading photos for
   this album. You can also add more photos after you create your
   album.

8. Click the **Create Album** button in the lower-right corner of the
   dialog box.

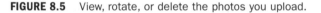

FIGURE 8.5   View, rotate, or delete the photos you upload.

9. In the **Share Album** dialog box, you can choose the people and circles you want to share your album with. You can share your album now or share it at a later time. Sharing an album displays it on the Google+ stream of everyone you share with. See "Sharing an Album" later in this lesson for more information. If you don't want to share this album right now, click the **Cancel** button.

Your new album now displays on the **Your Albums** tab on the **Photos** page. See "Viewing Your Photo Albums" later in this lesson for more information about this tab.

Viewing Your Photo Albums

To view your photo albums, click the **Photos** icon at the top of Google+ and select the **Your Albums** tab.

On this tab, you can:

▶ View a collection of photos from your posts, your profile photos, your scrapbook photos, and your photo albums. Figure 8.6 shows a sample of the **Your Albums** tab.

FIGURE 8.6   View all your photo albums in one place.

▶ Determine who you're sharing the album with by looking at the small icon next to each album. Pause your mouse over the icon to view its description. For example, a red circle with a diagonal line means that only you can view this album.

▶ Click an album to view the photos it contains. In the album, click an individual photo to open it in lightbox view where you can edit it.

▶ Rename an album. Click an album to open its detail page where you can enter a new album name in the text box.

Sharing an Album

You can share a photo album when you create it or at any time after that.

To share a photo album, follow these steps:

1. Click the **Photos** icon at the top of Google+.

2. On the left side of the page, click the **Your Albums** tab.

3. Select the album you want to share.

4. Click the **Share Album** button on the album detail page, as shown in Figure 8.7.

FIGURE 8.7   Share your photo album with others on Google+.

5. In the **Share Album** dialog box (see Figure 8.8), enter any introductory text about your album in the text box. For example, you could explain where you took these photos, why you're posting them, or what feedback you want from the people you're sharing with.

FIGURE 8.8   Choose exactly who you want to share with.

6. Specify who you want to share this album with. By default, Google+ displays your most recent sharing choices. For example, if you last shared a post with your Friends circle, that's what dis-

plays here. You can share with this same group of people or click the **Add More People** link to select other people to share with. For example, you can share with the people in one or more circles, your extended circles (friends of friends), the general public, or one specific person (enter this person's name in the text box). For a reminder on how to share on Google+, see Lesson 5.

7. Click the **Share** button to post your album on the stream, where only the people you shared with can view it. Figure 8.9 shows a sample shared album.

FIGURE 8.9   Display your album on the Google+ stream.

Deleting an Album

If you no longer want to keep a photo album or made a mistake and want to start over, you can delete it.

To delete a photo album, follow these steps:

1. Click the **Photos** icon at the top of Google+.

2. On the left side of the page, click the **Your Albums** tab.

3. Select the album you want to delete.

4. Click the **Delete Album** button on the album detail page (refer to Figure 8.7).

5. Click the **Delete** button in the dialog box that opens to confirm that you want to delete this album. Google+ permanently deletes the album.

Adding Photos to an Existing Album

You can add photos to any existing photo album, following a process very similar to creating your initial album.

To add more photos to an existing album, follow these steps:

1. Click the **Photos** icon at the top of Google+.

2. On the left side of the page, click the **Your Albums** tab.

3. Select the album to which you want to add more photos.

4. Click the **Add More Photos** button on the album detail page (see Figure 8.10).

FIGURE 8.10   Update an existing album with additional photos.

5. Click the **Select Photos from Your Computer** button.

6. In the **Choose File to Upload** dialog box, select the photo you want to add and click the **Open** button. Depending on your operating system and browser, this dialog box and button might have different names.

7. The **Add Photos** dialog box displays this photo, shown in Figure 8.10. Optionally, click the photo to add a caption, rotate it left or right, or delete it. You can also edit photos using the lightbox.

8. Click the **Upload More** link to continue uploading photos for this album.

9. Click the **Add Photos** button in the lower-right corner of the dialog box.

10. In the **Share Album** dialog box, you can choose the people and circles you want to share your updated album with. You can share your album now or share it at a later time. See "Sharing an Album" earlier in this lesson for more information. If you don't want to share this album right now, click the **Cancel** button.

Your updated album appears on the **Your Albums** tab on the **Photos** page. You might have to open your album again to view the new photos.

Working in the Photo Lightbox

The Google+ photo lightbox enables you to view, tag, caption, comment on, edit, delete, and manage your photos. Click a photo to open it in lightbox view, shown in Figure 8.11.

You can click a photo in your stream, on any of the tabs on the **Photos** page, or on your profile's **Photos** tab. The editing features available depend on whether you uploaded the photo or someone else did.

FIGURE 8.11   Lightbox view enables you to manage and edit photos.

Exploring the Lightbox

In lightbox view, you can:

- ▶ **Scroll through album photos.** Click the large arrows to the left and right of a photo to scroll through an album with a large number of photos.

- ▶ **Add a comment.** Add your own commentary about the photo in the **Add a Comment** box in the upper-right corner of the light-box. Click the **Post Comment** button to post your comment.

- ▶ **Add a caption.** Click the **Add a Caption** link below a photo to open a text box where you can add your caption. Click outside the text box to save your data.

- ▶ **Add a tag.** Click the **Add Tag** button below a photo to add a tag to it. See "Tagging Photos" later in this lesson for more information.

- ▶ **View photo details.** Select **Photo Details** from the **Actions** drop-down list to view details about this photo such as its dimensions, file size, exposure, aperture, and more.

▶ **Rotate a photo to the left.** Select **Rotate Left** from the **Actions** drop-down list to rotate the photo 180 degrees to the left.

▶ **Rotate a photo to the right.** Select **Rotate Right** from the **Actions** drop-down list to rotate the photo 180 degrees to the right.

▶ **Edit a photo.** Select **Edit Photo** from the **Actions** drop-down list to display editing options on the right side of the page. See "Editing Photos" later in this lesson for more information.

▶ **Delete a photo.** Select **Delete Photo** from the Actions drop-down list to delete the photo. Click **OK** in the dialog box that opens to confirm permanent deletion.

▶ **Report or delete comments.** Select **Report or Delete Comments** from the **Actions** drop-down list. On the right side of the page (see Figure 8.12), click the **Delete** link below a comment to delete it or the **Report Comment** link below a comment to report it to Google+.

FIGURE 8.12   Delete or report any inappropriate photo comments.

NOTE: **You Can't Edit a Photo You Didn't Upload**

If you're viewing a photo in lightbox view that someone else uploaded, you can add a comment, add a tag, view photo details, and report abuse, but you can't edit or delete the photo.

Tagging Photos

Tagging photos offers a way to identify the people in them. You can tag yourself and other people in photos. Google+ also gives you complete control over how and when others can tag you.

Tagging a Photo

To tag yourself or someone else in a photo, follow these steps:

1. Click a photo to open it in lightbox view.

2. Click the **Add Tag** button, shown in Figure 8.13.

FIGURE 8.13   Tag photos in lightbox view.

NOTE: **Google+ Recognizes Photos with People**

If you pause your mouse over a photo that includes people, Google+ displays a box around each person's face. Click the **Click to Name** text box below each person to tag that person. Automatic recognition doesn't work for all photos, but you can also tag a photo manually.

---

3. Drag the box with the dotted line to frame the person's face.

4. Start typing the name of the person you want to tag and select from the menu of Google+ users provided, as shown in Figure 8.14.

5. Click the **Close** (x) button in the upper-right corner of the screen to close the photo in lightbox view.

FIGURE 8.14   Select the name of a Google+ user to tag this photo.

If you tag a photo of yourself, it displays on the **Photos of You** tab on the **Photos** page.

If you tag a photo of someone else, that person is notified of your tag and has the option to approve or remove the tag.

Approving or Removing a Tag

When someone tags you in a photo, Google+ sends you a notification about this tag, allowing you to approve or remove it. By default, Google+ automatically approves tags from people in your circles. You can change this option, however. See "Specifying Photo Tag Approval Settings" later in this lesson for more information.

To respond to a photo tag notification, follow these steps.

1. Click the **Home** icon at the top of Google+ if you aren't already on your home page.

2. Click the **Notifications** link on the left side of the page.

NOTE: **View Photo Tag Notifications from the Google+ Bar**

Alternatively, you can also view and manage photo tag notifications by clicking the **Notifications** button on the Google+ bar.

---

3. Scroll down to the photo notification you want to review.

TIP: **Filter to Display Only All Photo Tag Notifications**

To display only your photo tag notifications, select **Photo Tags** from the **More** drop-down list in the upper-right corner of the **Notifications** page.

4. Google+ displays the current status of the tag below the photo. For example, in Figure 8.15, the tag is already approved because someone in one of your circles added it. If you want to accept the photo tag, you don't need to do anything. If you want to remove the photo tag, click the **Remove** button.

FIGURE 8.15   You can accept or remove photo tags.

Google+ displays photos tagged with your name on the **Photos of You** tab on the **Photos** page.

Removing a Photo Tag in Lightbox View

You can also remove photo tags in lightbox view.

To do so, follow these steps:

1. Click a photo to open it in lightbox view.

2. Click the **Remove Tag** link next to the tag you want to remove in the lower-right corner of the page.

In this photo: Patrice-Anne
Rutledge (photos | remove tag)

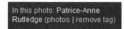

FIGURE 8.16 Remove photo tags in lightbox view.

3. Click the **OK** button in the dialog box that opens to confirm deletion.

Specifying Photo Tag Approval Settings

By default, Google+ automatically approves photo tags from anyone in your circles. You can change this default setting, however.

To specify whose tags you want Google+ to automatically approve, follow these steps:

1. Click the **Options** button in the upper-right corner of the Google+ bar and select **Google+ Settings** from the drop-down menu.
2. Scroll down the Google+ tab to locate the **Photos** section at the bottom of the page, as shown in Figure 8.17.

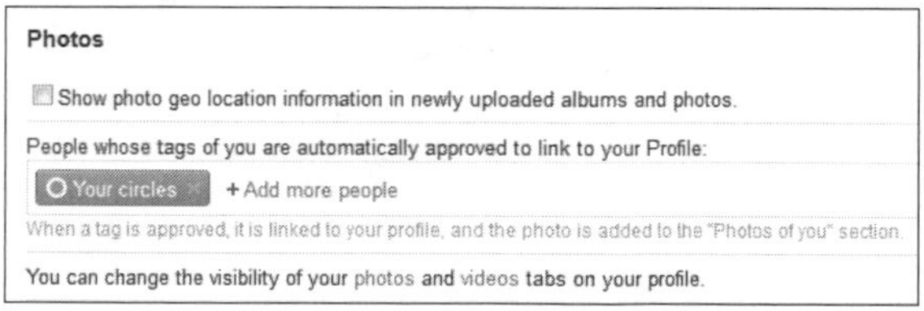

Photos
Show photo geo location information in newly uploaded albums and photos.
People whose tags of you are automatically approved to link to your Profile:
Your circles
+ Add more people
When a tag is approved, it is linked to your profile, and the photo is added to the "Photos of you" section.
You can change the visibility of your photos and videos tabs on your profile.

FIGURE 8.17 You're in control of the photo tags Google+ automatically approves.

3. Click the **Remove** icon (x) to the right of the **Your Circles** chip to require your manual approval for a photo tag. Google+ sends you a notification about any tag requiring approval and also displays pending tag approvals on the **Photos of You** tab on the **Photos** page.

> TIP: **Automatically Approve the Photo Tags Only of People in Specific Circles**
>
> If you want to give only certain circles automatic approval, click the **Add More People** link and select the appropriate circles. For example, you might want to automatically approve everyone in the Family and Friends circles, but not the Acquaintances or Following circles.

Google+ requires your approval anytime someone tags you whose tags aren't preapproved. See "Approving or Removing a Tag" earlier in this lesson for more information.

You can also specify photo tag approval settings when you edit the Photos tab on your profile.

Editing Photos

Google+ enables you to apply special effects and improve the quality of photos you upload.

> TIP: **Apply Additional Photo Effects in Picasa Web Albums**
>
> If you want to apply additional effects, check out the options in Picasa Web Albums (click the **Photos** link on the Google+ bar to access this application).

To edit a photo, follow these steps:

1. Select a photo to open it in lightbox view.

2. Select **Edit Photo** from the **Actions** drop-down list to display editing options on the right side of the page (see Figure 8.18).

3. Select an effect to apply it to your photo. Your options include:

    ▶ **Cross Process.** Apply an effect that simulates the processing of one type of film using a solution designed for another film type, resulting in strong, high-contrast colors.

    ▶ **Orton.** Blend two versions of the same photo using different exposures.

FIGURE 8.18   Apply effects to your photos.

> ▶ **I'm Feeling Lucky.** Apply a random effect.

> ▶ **Black and White.** Convert a color photo to black white.

> ▶ **Auto Color.** Adjust photo colors automatically.

> ▶ **Auto Contrast.** Adjust photo contrast automatically.

4. If you don't like the effect, click the **Undo** button and try a different effect.

5. If you're satisfied with the effect you applied, click the **Done Editing** button.

Working with Photo Scrapbooks

Google+ gives you the option of displaying favorite photos at the top of your profile through the use of photo scrapbooks. Figure 8.19 shows a sample photo scrapbook at the top of a profile.

FIGURE 8.19   Display five pre-selected photos at the top of your profile.

> **CAUTION: Consider Carefully Which Photos Are Appropriate for Your Scrapbook**
>
> Displaying a public photo scrapbook at the top of your profile is optional. If you do decide to use this feature, consider carefully the photos you want to represent you and display to the public. For example, I use my profile photo scrapbook to display cover photos of my recent books.

Adding a Photo Scrapbook to Your Profile

To add a photo scrapbook to your profile, follow these steps:

1. Click the **Profile** icon at the top of Google+.

2. Click the **Edit Profile** button in the upper-right corner of the page.

3. Click the **Add Some Photos Here** button at the top of your profile (see Figure 8.20).

FIGURE 8.20   Add up to five photos at the top of your profile.

4. Click the **Add Photo** link (see Figure 8.21) to open the **Add Photos to Scrapbook** dialog box.

FIGURE 8.21 Add photos you already uploaded to your scrapbook or upload new photos.

  5. Click the **Browse** button to select photos to upload. You can upload photos in the following formats: JPG, GIF, or PNG.

TIP: **Add Existing Google+ Photos to Your Scrapbook**

To add any of your existing photos on Google+ to your scrapbook, click the **Your Photos** tab on the **Add Photos to Scrapbook** dialog box, select a photo, and click the **Add Photos to Scrapbook** button.

---

  6. In the **Choose File to Upload** dialog box, select a file to upload and click the **Open** button. Depending on your operating system and browser, the name of this dialog box and button could vary.

  7. Continue uploading any additional photos. Google+ can display up to five photos on your profile.

  8. Click the **OK** button to close the scrapbook area.

  9. Click the **Done Editing** button at the top of your profile.

Your scrapbook photos are now available in the Scrapbook Photos album on the **Your Albums** tab on the **Photos** page.

TIP: **Rearrange the Display Order of Your Scrapbook in Picasa Web Albums**

To rearrange the display order of the photos in your scrapbook, click the **Photos** link on the Google+ bar to open Picasa Web Albums. Select your scrapbook in Picasa and click the **Organize** tab to rearrange photos.

Deleting a Scrapbook Photo

To delete a scrapbook photo, follow these steps:

1. Click the **Profile** icon at the top of Google+.

2. Click the **Edit Profile** button in the upper-right corner of the page.

3. Select the photo you want to delete and click the **Delete Photo** link that displays (see Figure 8.22).

Delete Photo link

FIGURE 8.22   Delete scrapbook photos if you want to add new ones.

4. Click the **OK** button in the dialog box that opens to confirm deletion.

5. Click the **OK** button to close the scrapbook area.

6. Click the **Done Editing** button at the top of your profile.

After deleting a photo, you can add a new photo to replace it.

Summary

In this lesson, you learned how to upload, manage, and edit photos in Google+. Next, get chatting with Google+ Chat.

LESSON 9

Chatting on Google+

In this lesson, you learn how to chat on Google+, using text, voice, and video.

Understanding Google+ Chat

Google+ enables you to communicate directly with other users through its chat functionality. You can chat in a text-based chat window, optionally enhanced with voice chat, video chat, or group chat.

Unlike other social sites such as Facebook, Google+ doesn't display everyone in your circles on your chat list, even if they are online on Google+. In order to chat with people on Google+, you must already chat with them using another Google product or invite them to chat.

Exploring the Chat List

If you use chat in other Google products such as Gmail, iGoogle, Google Talk, or Orkut, the people you've chatted with display in your chat list on the left side of your Google+ home page (see Figure 9.1).

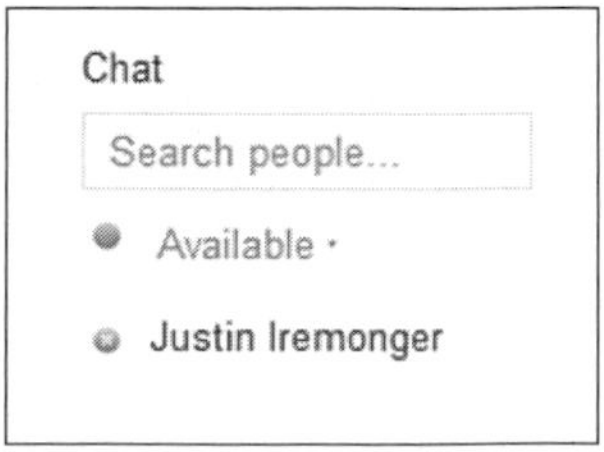

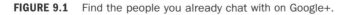

FIGURE 9.1   Find the people you already chat with on Google+.

If you don't use chat in any of these products, no one displays in your chat list yet. Instead, you must invite people to chat with you on Google+. See "Inviting People to Chat" later in this lesson.

Google+ uses color-coded icons to communicate the availability of the people you chat with:

▶ **Green.** Online and available to chat.

▶ **Yellow.** Idle. Google+ automatically switches a person's status to idle after 15 minutes of inactivity.

▶ **Red.** Busy (online, but unavailable to chat). Google+ users can display this status if they don't want to chat with others. For example, people who are at work might not be available to chat with friends.

▶ **Grey.** Offline or signed out of chat. Google+ users can display this status by selecting the Invisible status, even if they are still online.

See "Specifying Your Chat Availability" later in this lesson for more information about how to manually change your own status.

If you haven't enabled voice and video chat, availability is designated by a color-coded circle (refer to Figure 9.1). If you have enabled voice and video chat (either in Google+ or another Google product), the circle becomes a color-coded video icon, as shown in Figure 9.2.

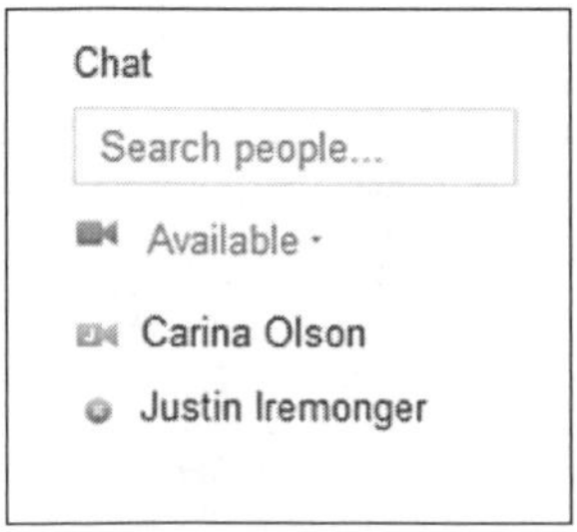

FIGURE 9.2   The video icon lets you know whether your computer is set up for video chat.

See "Using Voice and Video Chat" later in this lesson for more information about enabling this feature.

> TIP: **What Does That Icon Mean?**
> If you aren't sure what a color or icon means, pause your mouse over it to display a definition.

Specifying Your Chat Availability

By default, you're listed as available in the chat list (refer to Figure 9.1).

To change your availability status, click the **Available** link and select one of the following options from the drop-down menu (see Figure 9.3):

- ▶ Available (the default)

- ▶ Busy

- ▶ Invisible (changes your status to Offline)

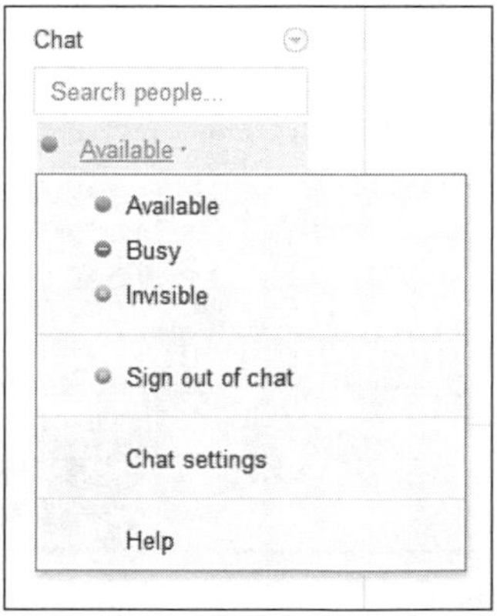

FIGURE 9.3   Your're in control of the chat availability you display to other Google+ users.

Inviting People to Chat

If you want to chat with someone who isn't already in your chat list, you must invite this person.

CAUTION: **You Can Invite Only People Who Use Google+**

People must already have a Google+ account before you can chat with them. If the individuals you want to chat with aren't on Google+, you must invite them to Google+ first and then invite them to chat after they join. See Lesson 3, "Managing Your Network with Circles" for more information about inviting people to Google+.

To invite another Google+ user to chat, follow these steps:

1. Click the **Home** icon at the top of Google+ if you aren't already on the home page.

2. Enter the name of the person you want to invite.

   ▶ For people who are already one of your contacts on a Google product (such as a Gmail contact), Google+ displays matching names from your contact list as you type (see Figure 9.4). Select the person you want to invite from the list.

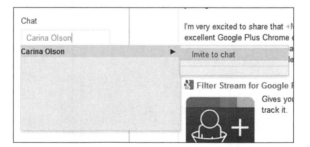

FIGURE 9.4   Google+ helps you find your contacts on other Google products.

   ▶ For people who aren't existing Google contacts, enter the email address associated with their Google+ account rather than a full name. Figure 9.5 shows an example of entering an email address.

3. Select **Invite to Chat** from the menu that opens.

FIGURE 9.5 Use an email address to connect with other Google+ users on chat.

4. Google+ alerts you that the person you're inviting must accept your invitation to chat and that your email address will be shared. Depending on the email service the invited person uses, the pop-up box could display either this person's actual email address or an encrypted one. If you agree to share your email address, click the **Send Invite** button. Figure 9.6 shows this button.

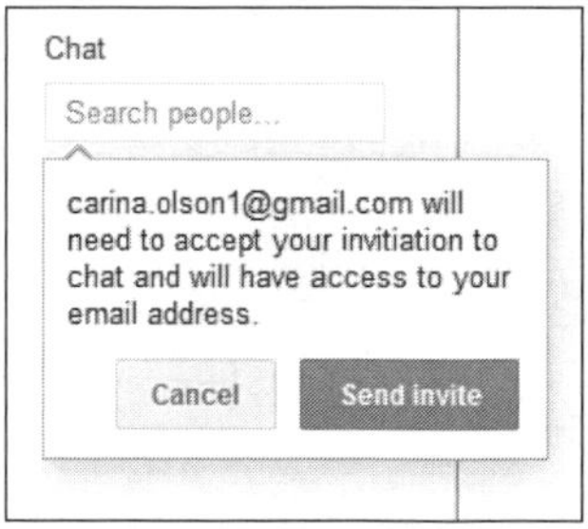

FIGURE 9.6 If you agree to share your email address, click the **Send Invite** button.

Google+ confirms that your invite was sent, as shown in Figure 9.7.

A message displays on the Google+ home page of the person you invited, prompting this person to click the **Yes** button to accept. As soon as someone accepts your invitation to chat, you display on each other's chat list and can begin chatting on Google+. If the person you invited doesn't accept your invitation, you won't be able to chat. In other words, you both must agree to chat before Google+ enables you to initiate chats with each other.

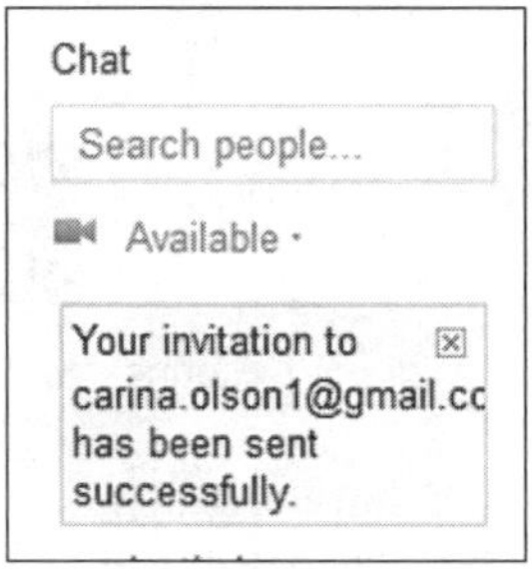

> Chat
>
> Search people...
>
> ■◀ Available ·
>
> Your invitation to   ☒
> carina.olson1@gmail.cc
> has been sent
> successfully.

FIGURE 9.7   After sending an invite, you must wait for a response.

NOTE: Why Is Google+ Saying My Invite Is Invalid?

If Google+ can't find the person you're trying to invite, you receive an alert (see Figure 9.8). This can happen for several reasons, such as the person you invited isn't on Google+ yet. You can also receive this message if you entered the full name of a person who isn't one of your Google contacts. In this case, you would need to use an email address to invite a Google+ user who isn't an existing contact. For example, if Anne Smith is on Google+, but isn't one of your Google contacts, you must send an invite to her email address, and not simply type her name in the text box.

> Chat
>
> |earch people...
>
> ■◀ Available ·
>
> Oops, Maria Clark   ☒
> looked invalid.
> Double check the
> address and try again.

FIGURE 9.8   If Google+ can't find the person you want to invite, an alert displays on your chat list.

Chatting on Google+

Google+ offers several options for chatting. You can participate in a text-based chat or enhance your conversation with voice and video chat. If you want to chat with more than one person, you can use group chat to participate in a text-based chat with an unlimited number of Google+ users.

Participating in a Chat

To chat with someone in your chat list, follow these steps:

1. Click the **Home** icon at the top of Google+ if you aren't already on the home page.

2. Click the name of the person you want to chat with in the chat list, as shown in Figure 9.9. A green icon displays before the names of people available to chat. See "Exploring the Chat List" earlier in this lesson for more information about the other icons in this list.

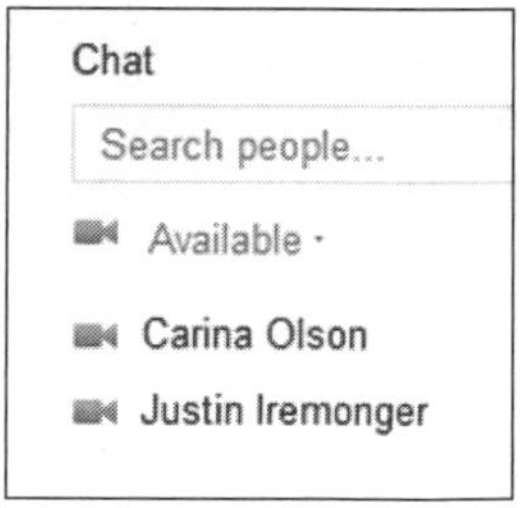

FIGURE 9.9   Your chat list displays people who have accepted your invitation to chat.

> **NOTE: The Person I Want to Chat with Isn't on the Chat List**
>
> If you want to chat with someone who doesn't display on your chat list, you must invite this person. See "Inviting People to Chat" earlier in this lesson for more information.

3. The chat window opens in the lower-right corner of the screen (see Figure 9.10). Type your chat message in the text box and

press the Enter key. Your message displays in the chat window of your recipient, who can then respond to you (see Figure 9.11).

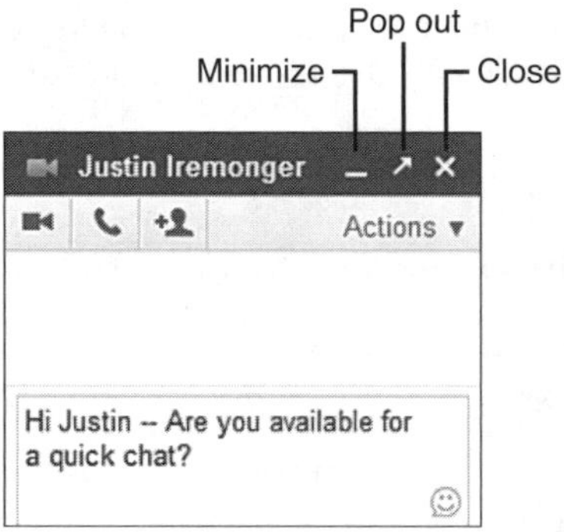

FIGURE 9.10 Conduct chats in the chat window, which displays in the lower-right corner of your screen.

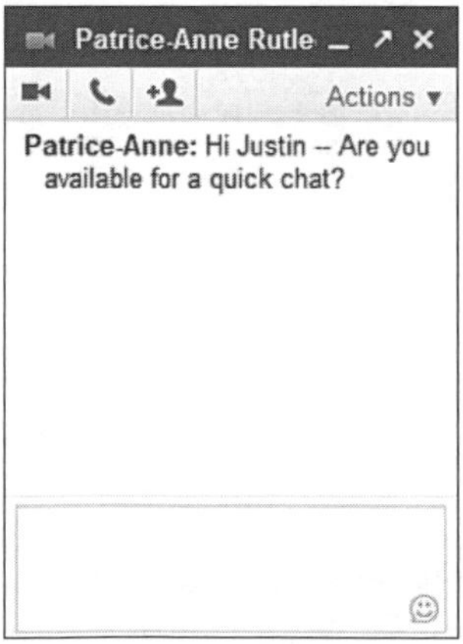

FIGURE 9.11 Your message as your recipient sees it.

4. When you're finished chatting, click the **Close (x)** icon in the upper-right corner of the chat window.

During your chat, you can:

▶ Minimize the chat window when you're not actively chatting by clicking the **Minimize** icon in the upper-right corner of the chat window.

▶ Open a separate window for chatting by clicking the **Pop-out** icon in the upper-right corner of the chat window.

▶ Use emoticons in your chat, such as a smiley face, sad face, or heart. To do so, click the smiley face icon in the lower-right corner on the chat window. A pop-up box with numerous emoticon possibilities opens, as shown in Figure 9.12. You can select any of these to add a personal touch to your chats. Google+ converts any text-based emoticon you enter—such as ":-)" to create a smiley face—to a graphic icon in your chat.

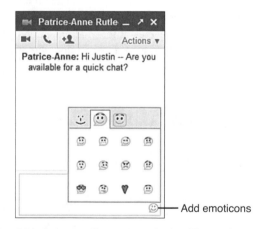

FIGURE 9.12   Add some emotion to text chats with emoticons.

Sending a File

If you're discussing a file with someone on Google+, you can send the file to this person via the chat window. For example, you can send Word documents, presentations, spreadsheets, or photos to another Google+ user.

To a send a file from the chat window, follow these steps:

1. In the chat window, select **Send a File** from the **Actions** drop-down list (see Figure 9.13).

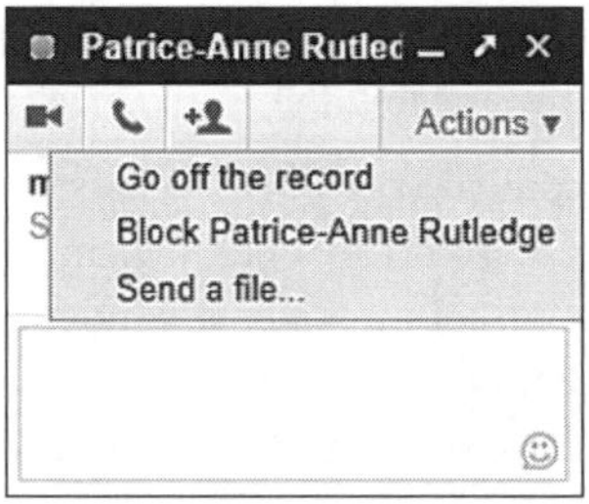

FIGURE 9.13   Send files to the people you chat with.

2. In the **Choose File to Upload** dialog box, select the file you want to send and click the **Open** button. Depending on your operating system and browser, the names of this dialog box and button could vary. The Chat window notifies you that you're sharing a file, as shown in Figure 9.14.

FIGURE 9.14   The chat window lets you know your file was sent.

3. Google+ alerts the recipient of the file, prompting this person to click the **Accept** link to open or save it. Figure 9.15 shows this from the recipient's view.

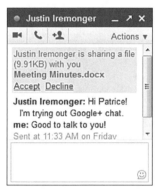

FIGURE 9.15   Your recipient must accept your file before viewing it.

4. When the recipient accepts your file, the chat window alerts you (see Figure 9.16).

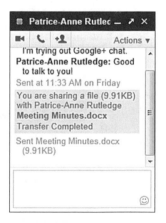

FIGURE 9.16   The chat window lets you know when the recipient accepts the file you sent.

Using Voice and Video Chat

You can add free, computer-to-computer voice and video chat to your Google+ chats using a simple plugin. This plugin requires one of the following operating systems:

► Windows XP Service Pack 3 or later

► Intel Mac OS X 10.5 or later

► Linux

In addition, you also need a microphone, speakers, and webcam to use voice and video chat.

If you use chat using another Google product such as Gmail or iGoogle, you might already have this plugin installed. If not, you can set it up from the Google+ chat window.

NOTE: **Check Out Google+ Hangouts for Video Chat**

If you want to participate in video chats, also check out Google+ Hangouts. See Lesson 10, "Using Hangouts for Video Chat," for more information.

Setting Up Voice and Video Chat

To add voice and video chat, follow these steps:

1. In the chat window, click the **Start Voice Chat** icon (see Figure 9.17).

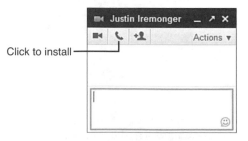

FIGURE 9.17   Setting up voice and video chat gives you more chat options.

2. Click the **Click Here** link to add voice and video chat.

3. The **Chat Face to Face with Family and Friends** page opens in a new window (see Figure 9.18). Click the **Install Voice and Video Chat** button to install this plugin. You might have to click the **Allow** button to continue installation.

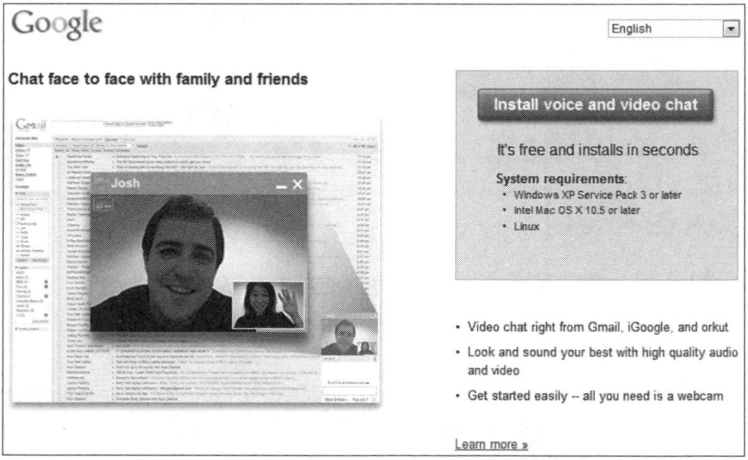

FIGURE 9.18   Click the Install Voice and Video Chat button to get started.

4. After installation is complete, close your browser and sign back in again.

5. On the left side of the home page, hover your mouse over **Chat** and click the down arrow to the right. Select **Settings** from the menu.

6. In the **Chat Settings** dialog box, shown in Figure 9.19, click the **Verify Your Settings** link to verify that your camera, microphone, and speakers work properly. Optionally, you can select the appropriate camera, microphone, and speakers from the dropdown lists.

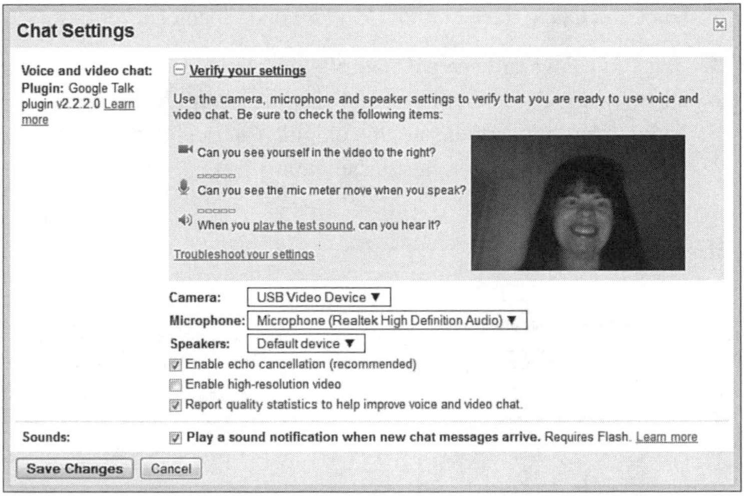

FIGURE 9.19   Verify your settings before starting to chat.

7. By default, Google+

   ▶ Enables echo cancellation, which helps reduce echo sounds during voice chats.

   ▶ Disables high-resolution video.

   ▶ Reports quality statistics to help improve voice and video chat.

   ▶ Plays a sound notification when new chat messages arrive (this feature requires Flash).

   You can retain these default settings or change them by selecting or deselecting the related checkbox.

8. Click the **Save Changes** button to save your changes and close the dialog box.

You're now ready to use voice and video chat. Google+ displays the video icon next to your status on the chat list (see Figure 9.20).

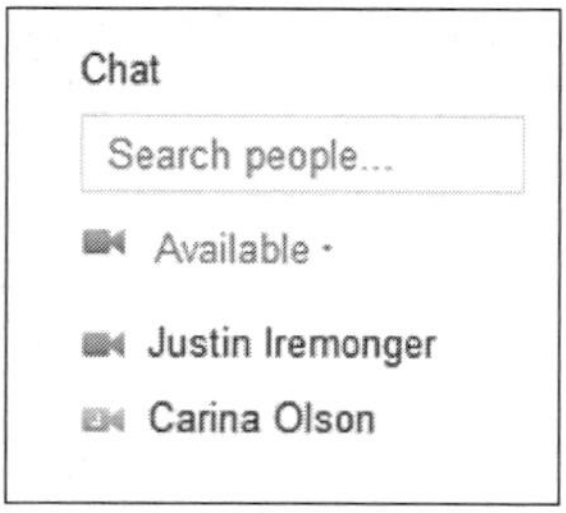

Chat

Search people...

◼◀ Available ·

◼◀ Justin Iremonger

◻◀ Carina Olson

FIGURE 9.20 The video icon shows that you enabled the voice and video plugin.

Participating in a Voice Chat

To add voice chat to an existing chat, follow these steps:

1. In the chat window, click the **Start Voice Chat** icon (see Figure 9.21).

Click to start
a voice chat

FIGURE 9.21 You can start a voice chat from the chat window.

2. Google+ alerts the person you're chatting with that you would like to start a voice chat, as shown in Figure 9.22. This person must have enabled the voice and video plugin and click the **Answer** button to participate in the call.

3. Conduct your voice chat.

4. When you're done talking, click the **End** button to end the voice chat.

5. Click the **Close (x)** icon in the upper-right corner of the chat window to close it.

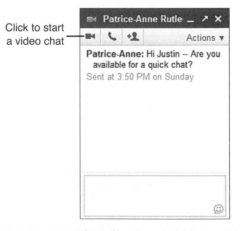

FIGURE 9.22   The person you want to talk with must answer your voice chat request.

Participating in a Video Chat

To add video chat to an existing chat, follow these steps:

1. In the chat window, click the **Start Video Chat** icon (see Figure 9.23).

FIGURE 9.23   Click the **Start Video Chat** icon to initiate a video chat.

2. Google+ alerts the person you're chatting with that you would like to start a video chat. This person must have enabled the voice and video plugin, have a webcam, and click the **Answer** button to participate in the video chat.

3. Conduct your video chat, as shown in Figure 9.24.

FIGURE 9.24   Participating in a video chat.

4. When you're done, click the **End** button to end the video chat.

5. Click the **Close (x)** icon in the upper-right corner of the chat window to close it.

Chatting Off the Record

By default, Google+ retains a record of your chats in Gmail. You must have a Gmail account to use this feature. To view a record of your Google+ chats with a Gmail contact, pause your mouse over this person's name in the Gmail chat list and select **Recent Conversations** from the **Video & More** drop-down menu (see Figure 9.25). If you haven't enabled video, this menu is called the **More** menu.

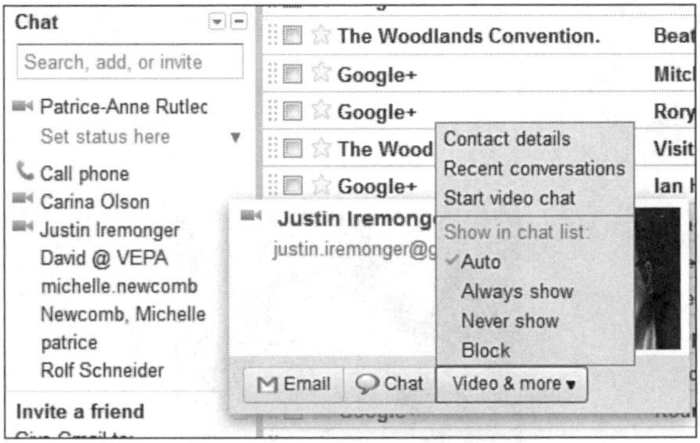

FIGURE 9.25 Google+ retains a record of your chats in Gmail.

If you don't want to save a record of your chats with someone, however, you can go off the record with that person. Google+ notifies the person you're chatting with when you choose to go off or on the record.

When chatting with someone in the chat window, select **Go Off the Record** from the **Actions** drop-down list (refer to Figure 9.26).

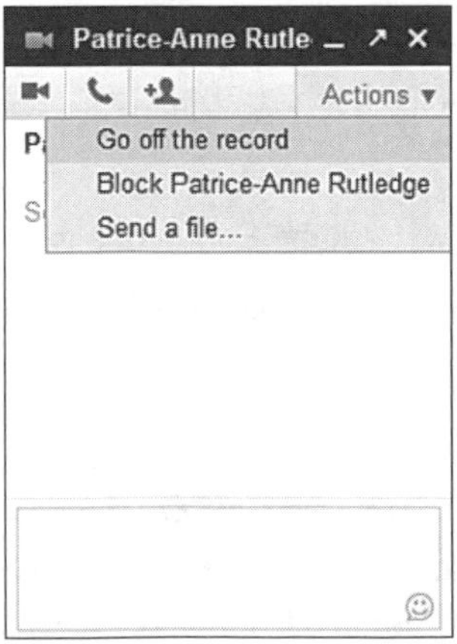

FIGURE 9.26 Go off the record if you don't want to record your Google+ chats with someone.

If you want to go back on the record again with this person, click the
Cancel link.

Starting a Group Chat

Group chat enables you to chat with an unlimited number of Google+
users at the same time.

NOTE: **Voice and Video Chat Aren't Available with Group Chats**
When you enter group chat, the **Start Video Chat** icon and **Start
Voice Chat** icon are no longer available in the chat window.

To start a group chat with people in your chat list, follow these steps:

1. Click the **Home** icon at the top of Google+ if you aren't already
   on the home page.

2. In the chat list, click the name of the first person you want to add
   to your group chat.

3. In the chat window, click the **Start Group Chat** icon (see
   Figure 9.27).

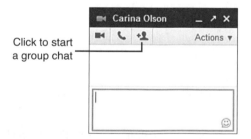

Click to start
a group chat

FIGURE 9.27 A group chat is just a click away.

4. In the **Add People to This Chat** text box, start typing the name
   of a person you want to add to the group chat. Google+ displays
   potential matches from your chat list as you type (see
   Figure 9.28).

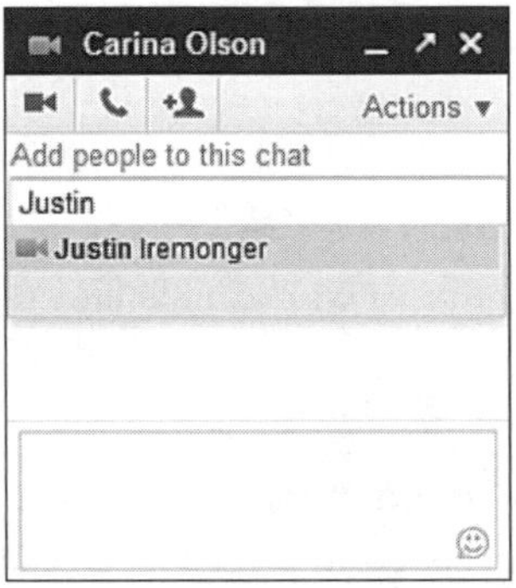

FIGURE 9.28   Add more people to your group chat.

5. Select the person you want from the list of options and click the **Invite** link. The chat window displays confirmation as each person joins the group chat, as shown in Figure 9.29.

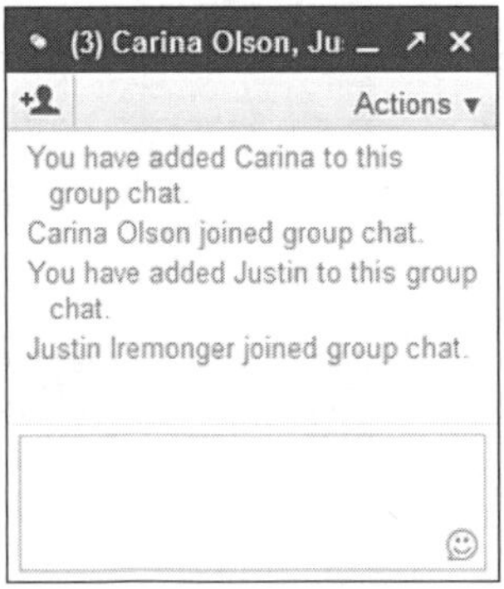

FIGURE 9.29   The chat window confirms the people who join the group chat.

6. Repeat steps 4 and 5 until all members of the group chat have joined.

7. Conduct your chat. Google+ displays the conversation of each person in the group, as shown in Figure 9.30.

8. When you're finished chatting, click the **Close (x)** icon in the upper-right corner of the chat window.

FIGURE 9.30   Participating in a group chat.

Blocking and Unblocking People on Chat

If you no longer want to chat with someone, you can block this person from starting chats with you. Blocking also prevents the blocked person from seeing you as available in the chat list. Any people you blocked from chatting in another Google product remain blocked in Google+.

> NOTE: **Blocking Someone on Chat Isn't the Same as Blocking Someone on Google+**
>
> The people you block from chatting with you remain in any circles you placed them. If you want to block someone entirely from Google+, this is a separate task. See Lesson 6, "Viewing Your Google+ Stream," for more information about blocking someone on Google+.

Blocking Someone from Chat

To block someone from chat, follow these steps:

   1. Click the **Home** icon at the top of Google+ if you aren't already on the home page.

   2. Select the name of the person you want to block in the chat list on the left side of the page.

> NOTE: **The Person I Want to Block Doesn't Display on My Chat List**
>
> If you want to block a Google contact you've never chatted with before, you need to search for this person. In the text box above the chat list, start typing the name of the person you want to block. Google+ displays matching names from your contact list as you type. Select the person you want to block from the list.

3. The chat window opens, listing the person you want to block.

> CAUTION: **Avoid Starting a Chat with Someone You Want to Block**
>
> To avoid initiating a chat with the person you want to block, don't type anything in the chat window text box.

4. In the chat window, select **Block [Full Name]** from the **Actions** drop-down list (see Figure 9.31).

FIGURE 9.31   Select the person you want to block.

The chat window notifies you that you've blocked this person. The chat window notifies you that you've blocked this person but doesn't notify the person you blocked. When blocked people try to initiate a chat with you, Google+ informs them that you cannot receive chat messages.

Unblocking Someone

If you block someone by mistake, or decide that you no longer want to block that person, you can unblock by clicking the **Unblock [Full Name]** link in the chat window.

To unblock someone later on, start typing this person's name in the text box above the chat list on the left side of the home page. Google+ displays matching names from your contact list as you type. Select the person you want to unblock and then select **Unblock** from the menu that opens.

> NOTE: **Unblocking in Google+ Chat doesn't Unblock from Other Google Products**
>
> If you blocked someone in another Google product, such as Gmail or Buzz, you must unblock this person in that product as well. Unblocking in Google+ doesn't carry over to other Google products.

Signing Out of Chat

You can sign out of chat completely and hide your availability from your contacts. (You'll display as Offline.) To do so, on the left side of the home page, hover your mouse over **Chat** and click the down arrow. Select **Sign Out** from the menu, as shown in Figure 9.32.

FIGURE 9.32   Sign out of chat when you don't want to display in the chat list of your Google+ friends.

You won't be able to chat again until you sign back into chat by clicking the **Sign Into Chat** link below the chat list. If you want to maintain a chat conversation with someone, but not be available to others, you should change your status to Invisible rather than sign out of Chat entirely.

> TIP: **Getting More Help with Google+ Chat**
>
> Although Google+ Chat is easy to use after you set it up, technical issues could complicate matters. If you follow the instructions in this lesson and still have problems with Chat, check out Google's troubleshooting tips at http://www.google.com/support/chat/bin/topic.py?hl=en&topic=24674.

Summary

In this lesson, you learned how to chat on Google+. Next, it's time to get visual with Google+ Hangouts for video chat.

LESSON 10

Using Hangouts for Video Chat

In this lesson, you learn how to use Google+ Hangouts to conduct a video chat.

Understanding Hangouts

Although Google+ offers many ways to share, connect, and collaborate with others, there are times when you just can't beat face to face communication. For those times, Google+ offers Hangouts.

> **PLAIN ENGLISH: Hangouts**
> Google+ Hangouts enable you to participate in live video chats with up to nine other Google+ users. Using Hangouts, you can casually chat with people in your circles or plan a hangout with specific people. You can also incorporate YouTube videos into your hangouts.

Preparing to Use Hangouts

Before getting started with Hangouts, be sure that you have all the required equipment, software, and plugins.

In order to participate in a hangout, you must:

▶ Use a computer with a 2Ghz dual core processor or greater and one of the following operating systems: Windows 7, Windows Vista, Windows XP, Mac OS X 10.5+, Chrome, or Linux.

▶ Have a webcam, microphone, and speakers. A headset is optional but produces better audio results.

▶ Use one of the following browsers: Google Chrome 10+, Microsoft Internet Explorer 8+, Mozilla Firefox 3+, or Safari 4+.

▶ Have bandwidth of 900kbps (up/down) for one-on-one hangouts or 900kbps/1800kbps (up/down) for group hangouts.

▶ Install Google's voice and video chat plugin. Lesson 9, "Chatting on Google+," described the installation of this plugin. If you haven't installed it, however, you can do so at www.google.com/chat/video.

NOTE: Can I Participate in a Hangout from a Mobile Device?

Currently, Hangouts works only on Android 2.3+ mobile devices with a front-facing camera using the Google+ Android app (https://market.android.com/details?id=com.google.android.apps.plus). Additional mobile devices will be supported over time. If you don't have a compatible phone, you must use a desktop or laptop computer to participate in a hangout. Another option is to create a Google+ Huddle for mobile group chat. See Lesson 12, "Using Google+ Mobile," for more information.

Starting a Hangout

To start a hangout, follow these steps:

1. Click the **Home** icon at the top of Google+ if you aren't already on the home page.

2. On the right side of the page, click the **Start a Hangout** button, as shown in Figure 10.1.

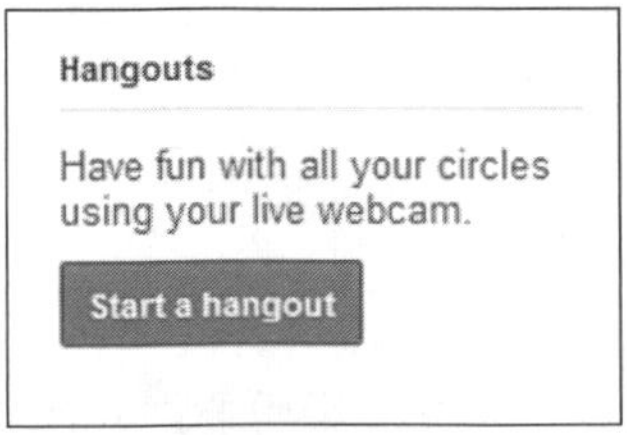

Hangouts

Have fun with all your circles using your live webcam.

Start a hangout

FIGURE 10.1   Hang out with friends on Google+.

TIP: Hang Out Directly from the Web

You can also go to http://plus.google.com/hangouts to access the Google+ Hangouts page.

3. Click the **Settings** button at the bottom of the Google+ Hangouts window, as shown in Figure 10.2.

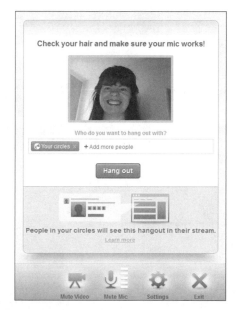

FIGURE 10.2   Set up Hangouts before using it the first time.

TIP: **Skip Setup If You've Already Used Hangouts**

If you've used Hangouts before and feel confident that your settings are accurate, you can skip steps 3 through 6. If you're new to Hangouts, however, these steps are essential.

---

4. In the **Settings** dialog box, shown in Figure 10.3, verify that your webcam, microphone, and speakers work properly. Optionally, you can select the appropriate camera, microphone, and speakers from the drop-down lists.

NOTE: **I'm Having a Setup Problem**

If you're having problems with your webcam or microphone, click the **Troubleshoot Your Settings** link in the **Settings** dialog box, which opens a page with troubleshooting tips. Common reasons for

---

Hangouts setup problems are not installing the voice and video chat plugin (www.google.com/chat/video), not turning up your microphone volume, or an outdated webcam driver.

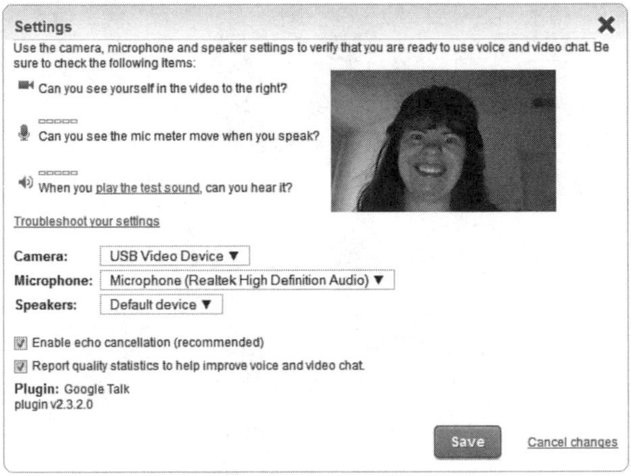

Settings

Use the camera, microphone and speaker settings to verify that you are ready to use voice and video chat. Be sure to check the following items:

■ Can you see yourself in the video to the right?

🎤 Can you see the mic meter move when you speak?

🔊 When you play the test sound, can you hear it?

Troubleshoot your settings

Camera: USB Video Device ▼

Microphone: Microphone (Realtek High Definition Audio) ▼

Speakers: Default device ▼

☑ Enable echo cancellation (recommended)

☑ Report quality statistics to help improve voice and video chat.

Plugin: Google Talk
plugin v2.3.2.0

Save   Cancel changes

FIGURE 10.3   Verify your settings before starting to hang out.

5. By default, Google+

   ▶ Enables echo cancellation, which helps reduce echo sounds during your hangout.

   ▶ Reports quality statistics to help improve voice and video chat.

   You can retain these default settings or change them by removing the checkmark next to the related checkbox.

6. Click the **Save** button to save your changes and close the dialog box.

7. Specify who you want to hang out with. Your options include the following:

   ▶ **Everyone in your circles.** By default, Google+ makes your hangout available to everyone in your circles. If you don't want to make this hangout available to this wide an audience, click the **Delete** icon (x) on the right side of the **Your Circes** button.

▶ **People in specific circles.** To hang out only with people in a specific circle or circles, click the **Add More People** link. In the menu that opens (see Figure 10.4), select the circle or circles you want to include. For example, you could start a hangout with family members, work friends, and so forth. When you're finished selecting circles, click outside the menu to close it.

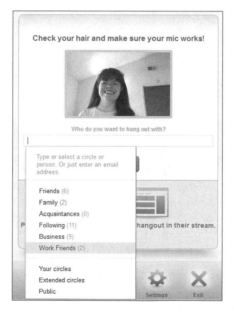

FIGURE 10.4   You can choose the specific circles and people you want to hang out with.

▶ **A specific person.** This enables you to start a private hangout with another Google+ user. Type the person's name in the text box and select from the pop-up menu of potential matches (see Figure 10.5).

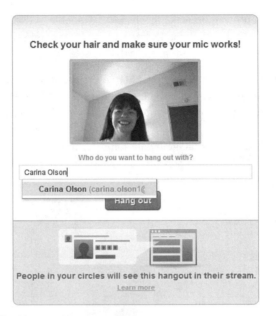

FIGURE 10.5   You can hang out with just one person.

CAUTION: Think Carefully About Who You Want to Hang Out With

Although you can choose to make your hangout available to your extended circles or even the general public, you should think twice before doing so. If someone you don't know or who is disruptive joins a hangout, you can't remove this person without ending the entire hangout. Because only 10 people can participate in a hangout at one time, hangouts are best suited to small group communication.

---

   8. Click the **Hang Out** button to open the Google+ Hangouts window (see Figure 10.6) where you can start your hangout.

Google+ alerts the people you chose to hang out with in step 7. As soon as they join, you can start participating in your hangout. See "Joining a Hangout" later in this lesson for more information about how people join a hangout.

FIGURE 10.6 Open the Google+ Hangouts window to start your hangout.

> NOTE: **My Hangout Isn't Working Properly**
>
> If you're having problems with a hangout, verify that you meet the system requirements specified in "Preparing to Use Hangouts" and that you tested your webcam, microphone, and speakers in step 4. If you did this and are still having problems, try closing any unnecessary programs you have open. If that doesn't work, end your hangout, restart your computer, and start a new hangout.

Inviting People to a Hangout

Once your hangout gets started, you—or anyone in your hangout—can always invite more people. Remember, however, that no matter how many people you invite, Google+ allows only 10 people in a hangout at one time.

To invite people to an in-progress hangout, follow these steps:

1. In the Google+ Hangouts window, click the **Invite** button in the lower-left corner (see Figure 10.7).

FIGURE 10.7 Invite more people to join the fun.

2. In the **Invite More People** box (see Figure 10.8), click the **Add Circles or People to Share With** link, select the circle or circles you want to invite, and click outside the menu to close it. Optionally, you can also enter the name of a specific person you want to hang out with.

Invite more people

＋Add circles or people to share with...

Invite

FIGURE 10.8   Select the people you want to add.

3. Click the **Invite** button to invite the selected people to the hangout.

Google+ alerts the people you invited to your hangout. See "Joining a Hangout" later in this lesson for more information about how people join a hangout.

Joining a Hangout

Google+ notifies you about hangouts in several ways, each of which enables you to easily join the hangout:

▶ If someone in one of your circles is hanging out, a post displays on your stream. Click the **Join This Hangout** button to participate. Figure 10.9 shows a sample post for a hangout.

FIGURE 10.9 Learn about hangouts from your Google+ stream.

▶ If someone in one of your circles is hanging out, Google+ sends you a notification. Click the **Notifications** button on the Google+ bar to open the **Notifications** menu, select the hangout notification (see Figure 10.10), and click the **Join This Hangout** button to join (see Figure 10.11).

FIGURE 10.10 Select the hangout notification you want to see.

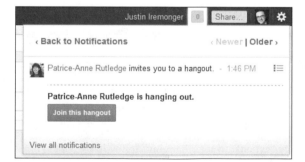

FIGURE 10.11 Join a hangout with the click of a button.

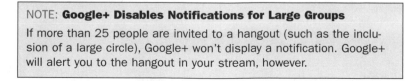

NOTE: **Google+ Disables Notifications for Large Groups**

If more than 25 people are invited to a hangout (such as the inclusion of a large circle), Google+ won't display a notification. Google+ will alert you to the hangout in your stream, however.

▶ If someone invites you personally to a hangout (selects your name rather than a circle you belong to), Google+ alerts you about the hangout in the chat window, shown in Figure 10.12. You must be signed in to chat to view this alert. Click the link to join the hangout or click the **Close** button (x) if you don't want to participate. If the hangout ends, the window closes automatically.

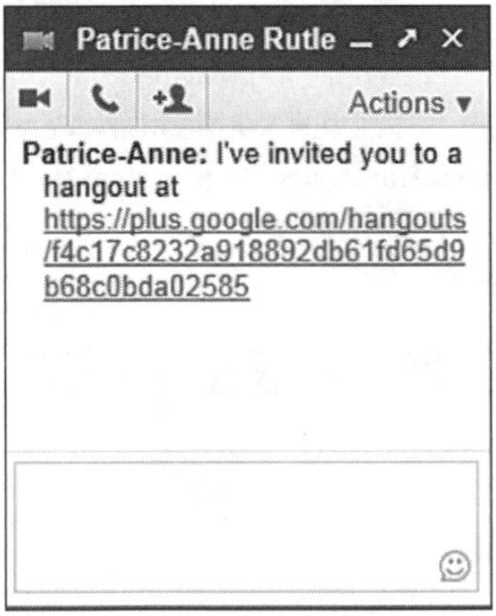

FIGURE 10.12   Learn about personal invitations to hang out in your chat window.

Adding Group Text Chat to a Hangout

You can add text-based chat to your hangout for another way to communicate with your group. Unlike traditional chats, Google+ doesn't retain a record of a chat conducted during a hangout.

To add group text chat to your hangout, follow these steps:

1. Click the **Chat** button in the lower left corner of the Google+ Hangouts window, as shown in Figure 10.13.

2. In the text box at the bottom of the chat window, type your text and press **Enter**. Google+ displays your text in the chat window

for everyone in the hangout to see, just as it does with a regular chat (see Figure 10.14).

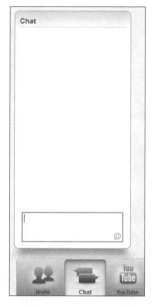

FIGURE 10.13   Add group text chat to your hangout.

3. Participate in group text chat during your hangout.

4. Click the **Chat** button again to close the chat window.

TIP: **Add Some Emotion to Your Group Text Chats**

You can add some emotion to your text with an emoticon, such as a smiley face, sad face, or heart. To do so, click the smiley face icon in the lower-right corner of the chat window. A pop-up box with numerous emoticon possibilities opens, as shown in Figure 10.15. You can select any of these to add a personal touch to your chats. Google+ also converts any text-based emoticon you enter—such as ":-)" to create a smiley face—to a graphic icon in your chat.

Chat

me: Welcome to the hangout!

FIGURE 10.14   Participating in group text chat.

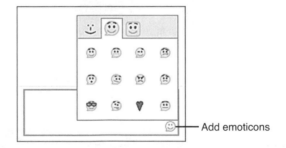

Add emoticons

FIGURE 10.15   Add emotion to your text chat with emoticons such as a smiley face.

Adding YouTube Video to Your Hangout

To add more interactivity to your hangouts, Google+ gives you the option of viewing YouTube videos while you're hanging out. Anyone in the hangout can play a YouTube video, not just the person who started the hangout.

To play a YouTube video during your hangout, follow these steps:

1. Click the **YouTube** button in the lower-left corner of the Google+ Hangouts window, as shown in Figure 10.16.

FIGURE 10.16 Enliven your hangouts with YouTube videos.

2. Type a search term in the search box in the upper-right corner of the screen and click the **Search** button. For example, you can search for your own videos by entering your name. Optionally, you can play one of the random videos that display in the **Featured Videos** section.

NOTE: **Why Can't I See the YouTube Video?**

You must use a current version of Google Chrome, Mozilla Firefox, or Microsoft Internet Explorer to view YouTube videos in Hangouts.

3. Select the video you want to play from the search results, as shown in Figure 10.17.

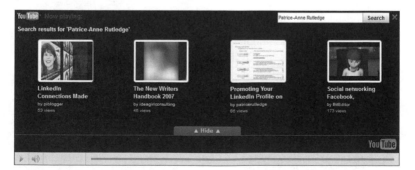

FIGURE 10.17 Select a YouTube video to play in your hangout.

4. Watch the video during your hangout (see Figure 10.18).

FIGURE 10.18   Watching a video during a hangout.

5. By default, Google+ mutes everyone in the hangout while the YouTube video plays. If you want to talk during the video playback, click the **Push to Talk** button. Alternatively, you can click the **Mute** button on the YouTube player, which mutes the video soundtrack and unmutes your hangout microphone.

6. Click the **Close** (x) button in the upper-right corner of the screen to close the video.

Muting During a Hangout

To control sounds and activity during a hangout, you can:

▶ Turn off your microphone by clicking the **Mute Mic** button in the lower-right corner of the Google+ Hangouts window, as shown in Figure 10.19. Google+ notifies the other people in your hangout that you're muted by displaying the **Mute** icon in the upper-right corner of your video thumbnail. For example, if you need to talk to someone else or answer the phone while you're in a hangout, you should mute yourself. You can return to the conversation by clicking the Unmute Mic button (see Figure 10.20).

FIGURE 10.19   Mute your microphone if you don't want people to hear what you say.

FIGURE 10.20   Unmute when you're ready to talk again.

▶ Mute a loud or boisterous hangout participant by pausing your mouse over this person's video thumbnail and clicking the **Remote Mute Participant** button in the lower-left corner (see Figure 10.21). Be aware, however, that muted participants can unmute themselves at any time.

FIGURE 10.21   Quiet down a loud hangout participant.

▶ Turn off your webcam by clicking the **Mute Video** button in the lower-right corner of the Google+ Hangouts window (refer to Figure 10.19). Google+ replaces your video thumbnail with a black screen until you click the **Unmute Video** button when you're camera-ready again, as shown in Figure 10.22.

FIGURE 10.22   Go black until you're ready to face the camera again.

Ending a Hangout

To end a hangout, click the **Exit** button in the lower-right corner of the Google+ Hangouts window (refer to Figure 10.19).

Using Hangouts with Extras

During its beta period, Google+ is previewing future Hangouts features. With Google+ Hangouts with Extras, you can

▶ **Name your hangout.** Naming your hangout is useful when you want to create a public broadcast.

▶ **Share your screen.** Share what's on your computer screen with others in your hangout, as shown in Figure 10.23.

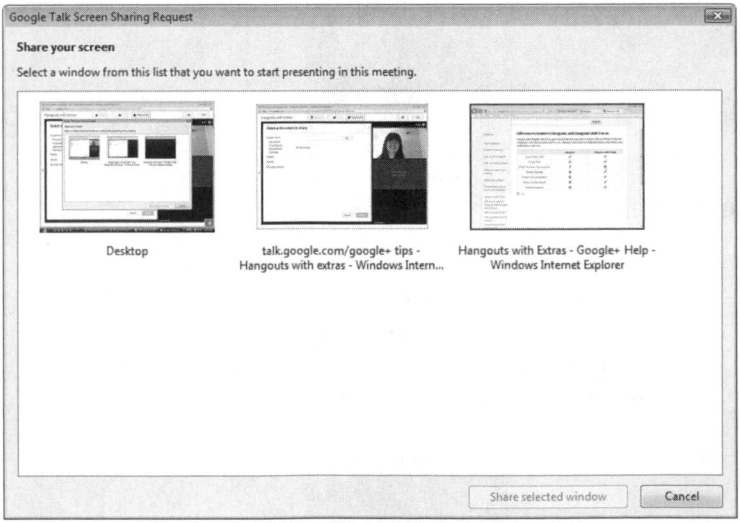

FIGURE 10.23   Select an open window you want to share with people in your hangout.

▶ **Collaborate with Google Docs.** View and collaborate on a document from Google Docs during your hangout (see Figure 10.24).

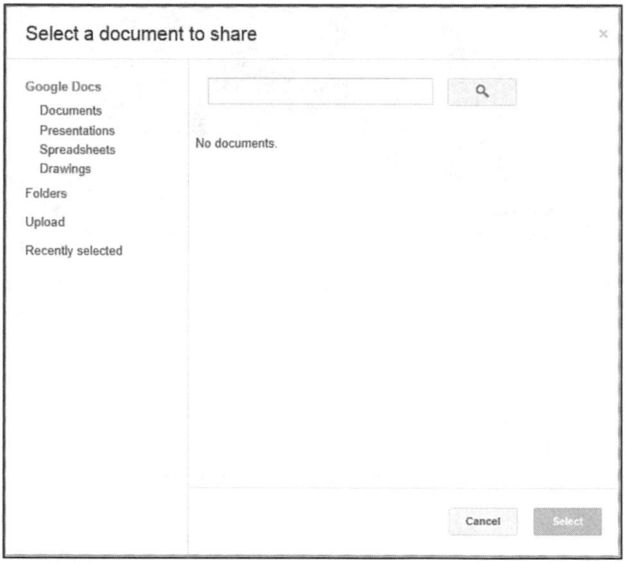

Select a document to share   ×

Google Docs
  Documents
  Presentations   No documents.
  Spreadsheets
  Drawings
Folders
Upload
Recently selected

                                                              Cancel   Select

FIGURE 10.24   Select a document from Google Docs to view in your hangout.

▶ **Take notes or draw on the Sketchpad.** Create live meeting minutes or collaborate on a writeboard during your hangout.

To access these features during the preview, click the **Hangouts with Extras** link on the **Hangouts** main window. After the preview, Google+ will integrate these features into Hangouts.

Using Google+ Hangouts on Air

With Google+ Hangouts on Air, you can produce a public broadcast. This feature enables you to start a hangout with up to 10 active participants and then choose to let anyone on the web watch your live broadcast (see Figure 10.25).

FIGURE 10.25   Produce a live web broadcast using Google+ Hangouts on Air. Source: http://googleblog.blogspot.com/2011/09/google-92-93-94-95-96-97-98-99-100.html.

During the beta, only selected users have the ability to create an on-air hangout, but Google+ plans to roll out Hangouts on Air over time to more users. Anyone can watch an on-air hangout, however.

Summary

In this lesson, you learned how to participate in video chat using Google+ Hangouts. Next, have some fun playing games on Google+.

LESSON 11

Playing Games

In this lesson, you learn how to have fun—and protect your privacy—while playing games on Google+.

Exploring Google+ Games

Google+ offers a variety of online and social games you can play, including Angry Birds, Zynga Poker, Sudoku Puzzles, Edgeworld, Bejeweled Blitz, and other popular games.

To view available games, click the **Games** icon at the top of Google+. Figure 11.1 shows this icon.

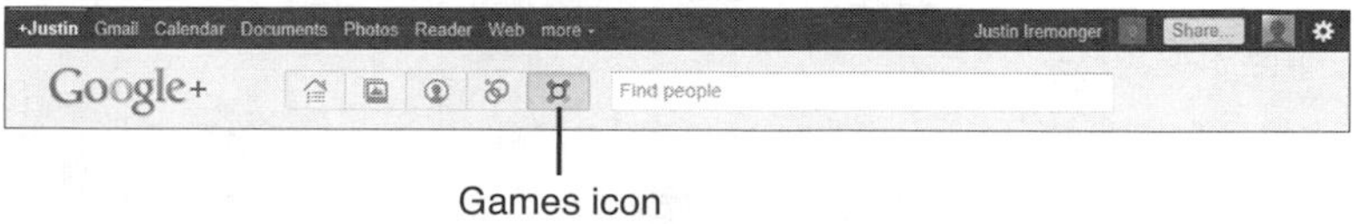

Games icon

FIGURE 11.1   Click the **Games** icon to get started with Google+ games.

On the Games page, you can view featured games as they scroll across your screen (see Figure 11.2).

Optionally, click the **All Games** link on the left side of the page to view a list of all available Google+ games, as shown in Figure 11.3.

FIGURE 11.2   The **Featured Games** tab previews popular Google+ games.

FIGURE 11.3   View all Google+ games on one page.

Playing a Game

Although each game on Google+ has different rules and objectives, the way you access a game is the same for all Google+ games.

To play a game on Google+, follow these steps:

  1. Click the **Games** icon at the top of Google+ (refer to Figure 11.1).

2. Click the **Play** button for a featured game to open that game (refer to Figure 11.2). Optionally, click the **All Games** link on the left side of the page, pause your mouse over a game's icon, and click the **Play** button (see Figure 11.4).

FIGURE 11.4 Click the **Play** button to open a game.

3. If you've never played that game before, Google+ opens the **Games in Google+ Are Social** dialog box. Figure 11.5 shows this dialog box, which lets you know how Google+ might share your gaming activity. Click the **Got It, Let's Play** button to continue.

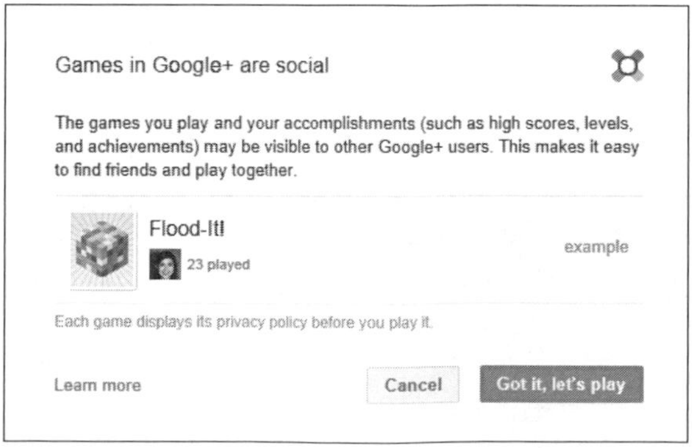

FIGURE 11.5 Google+ informs you that game activity can be public.

> NOTE: **What Personal Data Do Games Access and What Do They Do with It?**
>
> The personal data that games access varies by game. For example, a game could view basic information about your account, your email address, a list of people from your circles, and so forth. Google+ games could use this data to display your name and photo as a recent player on the Featured Games tab visible to people who have you in circles or list your name on a game leaderboard within a game.

4. Review what the game wants permission to access, shown in Figure 11.6, and click the **Allow Access** button to go to your game. Most games access your basic account information and the names of people in your circles, but some games access other data as well.

Google | Diamond Dash

Diamond Dash is requesting permission to:

‣ View basic information about your account

‣ View a list of people from your circles, ordered based on your interactions with them across Google

‣ More info

[Allow Access] [No thanks]

By proceeding, you agree to the application's Terms of Service and Privacy Policy.

FIGURE 11.6   Review what data the game accesses before agreeing to play.

> NOTE: **What Happens If I Don't Want to Give Google+ Permission to Access My Data?**
>
> If you click the **No Thanks** button, Google+ doesn't access your data and returns you to the main **Games** page. Refusing to give permission, however, means that you won't be able to play this game.

Figure 11.7 shows a sample Google+ game, Diamond Dash. Follow the on-screen directions and start playing your game.

FIGURE 11.7   Wait until your game loads and then start playing.

After you play a game, it displays in the **Recently Played** list on the
Games page, as shown in Figure 11.8. This gives you easy access to the
games you enjoy.

FIGURE 11.8   Access your favorite games from the Recently Played list.

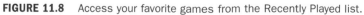

Sending Game Invitations and Requests

Many Google+ games allow you to invite friends to play or send other requests to friends. Although the way invitations and requests work vary by game, the process Google+ uses to notify people is the same.

As an example, let's see how the invitation process works on Bejeweled Blitz.

To invite a friend to play Bejeweled Blitz, follow these steps:

1. Click the **Games** icon at the top of Google+.

2. In the **Recently Played** section, click the **Bejeweled Blitz** link to open this game. If you haven't played this game before, click the **All Games** link and select the game on the **All Games** page. You must give permission to Google+ to play a game before you can invite others.

3. Click the **Invite Friends** button, shown in Figure 11.9.

FIGURE 11.9   Invite friends to play Google+ games.

4. In the **Select People** dialog box (see Figure 11.10), select the person or persons you want to invite. If you have a large network, you might need to search for the right people.

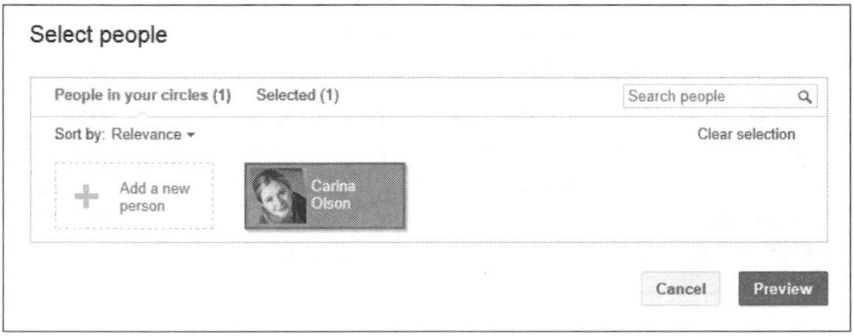

FIGURE 11.10   Invite people from your circles to play.

5. Click the **Preview** button to preview your invitation. Figure 11.11 shows the **Preview Your Message** dialog box, which opens.

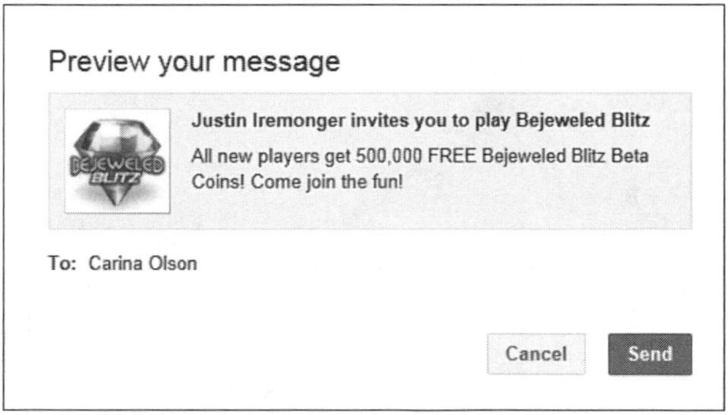

FIGURE 11.11   Preview your invitation before sending.

6. Click the **Send** button to send your invitation.

The people you invite receive your invitations on their **Game Notifications** page, where they can choose whether or not to respond. See "Viewing and Responding to Game Notifications" next in this lesson for more information about notifications.

Viewing and Responding to Game Notifications

When someone invites you to play a game, sends a game gift, or sends a game-related request, this notification displays on your **Game Notifications** page.

> NOTE: **Why Don't My Game Notifications Display on the Notifications Menu?**
>
> Rather than viewing game-related notifications on the **Notifications** menu you access from the Google+ bar, you view these notifications on the **Game Notifications** page instead. Google+ separates game notifications because most people want to separate their gaming activity from their regular Google+ activity.

To view and respond to game notifications, follow these steps:

1. Click the **Games** icon at the top of Google+.

2. Click the **Game Notifications** link on the left side of the Games page.

3. On the **Game Notifications** page (see Figure 11.12), you can do the following:

Click to hide notification
or report abuse

FIGURE 11.12   View all your game notifications in one place.

- ► Click the name of the person who sent you the invitation to view this person's Google+ profile.

- ► Click the **Play Now** link to accept the invitation and start playing the game.

- ► Click the down arrow in the upper-right corner of the notification and select **Hide This Notification** from the menu that opens. Google+ hides the notification from the **Notifications** page.

▶ Click the down arrow in the upper-right corner of the notification and select **Report Abuse** from the menu that opens.

CAUTION: **Consider Carefully When to Report a Notification as Abuse**

You can report notifications that violate Google+ terms and conditions (spam, nudity, hate speech, violence, copyright, or child abuse). If someone invites you to a game you don't want to play, you should just hide the notification. Game invitations don't constitute abuse unless someone repeatedly sends you invitations to the point of harassment.

Sharing Game Activity on the Games Stream

If you're active on Google+ games, you might want to share your gaming success with friends. Using the Games stream, you can publish game updates to those who are interested in such information while not cluttering your main Google+ stream with gaming news. For example, gaming friends might be interested in learning about your highest score ever on Bejeweled Blitz, but those in your Clients and Business Connections circles might not.

TIP: **Consider Creating a Circle for Gaming Friends**

If you play games frequently, consider creating a circle for the friends you play games with. That way, you can more precisely control who you share game updates with and not bother non-gaming friends with your news.

How you share varies by game, but in general, a game prompts you to click the **Share** button to share your game results or other game-related news on your Games stream. Remember, however, that sharing is optional. If you don't want to post your game results on the Games stream, don't click the **Share** button.

As an example, let's look at how to share the good news about your high score in Bejeweled Blitz.

To share an update from Bejeweled Blitz, follow these steps:

1. On the **Bejeweled Blitz** page informing you of your high score, click the **Share** button (see Figure 11.13).

FIGURE 11.13   Share the good news with gaming buddies.

2. Figure 11.14 shows the **Post** dialog box, which opens. Click the **Add Circles or People to Share With** link.

FIGURE 11.14   You control who views your game updates.

3. In the drop-down list that displays, shown in Figure 11.15, select the circles you want to share with.

FIGURE 11.15   Select the circles you want to share your game update with.

4. Click the **Post** button to share your game update.

Figure 11.16 shows your Games stream, which displays at the bottom on the Google+ Games page. This post also displays on the Games stream of the people you shared with.

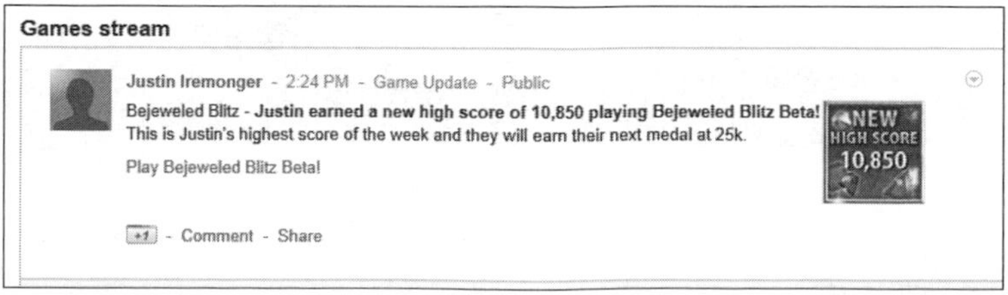

FIGURE 11.16   View game updates and news on the Games stream.

Posts in the Games stream are similar to posts on your regular stream, except that they are in a different location and you're able to share them with different circles, such as a circle just for your gaming friends. You can +1, comment on, or share posts in the Games stream on your regular stream. See Lesson 6, "Viewing Your Google+ Stream," for more information about managing posts in a stream.

Buying Virtual Goods

Some games on Google+ let you buy virtual goods. For example, you can purchase gold bars on City of Wonder or platinum on Edgeworld. If you decide to spend your hard-earned money on the purchase of virtual goods, you can do so through Google Checkout. Google Checkout enables you to pay for virtual goods using a credit card such as American Express, Visa, MasterCard, or Discover.

Although the goods you can buy and their price vary by game, Google+ processes these purchases in a similar way. As an example, let's look at the process for purchasing gold bars on City of Wonder.

To buy gold bars on City of Wonder, follow these steps:

1. Click the **Games** icon at the top of Google+.

2. In the **Recently Played** section, click the **City of Wonder** link to open this game, shown in Figure 11.17. If you haven't played this game before, click the **All Games** link and select the game on the **All Games** page. You must give permission to Google+ to play a game before you can buy virtual goods.

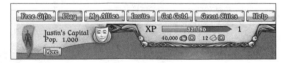

FIGURE 11.17   Buy gold bars on City of Wonder.

3. Click the **Get Gold** tab on the **City of Wonder** menu to open the Get Gold page (see Figure 11.18).

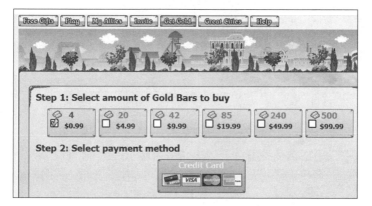

FIGURE 11.18   Choose from a variety of purchase options.

4. Select the number of gold bars you want to buy and click the **Credit Card** button.

5. In the pop-up box, click **Start Now** to sign in to your Google account.

6. On the **Google Checkout** page (see Figure 11.19), enter your credit card information and follow the steps listed to process your order.

Removing Game Permissions

If you decide you no longer want to play a game or no longer want a game to have access to your personal data, you can remove permissions for that game.

To remove game permissions, follow these steps:

1. Click the **Games** icon at the top of Google+.

2. In the **Recently Played** section, click the game whose permissions you want to remove. If the game doesn't display in this list, click the **All Games** link, pause your mouse over the game's icon, and click the **Play** button.

FIGURE 11.19   Use Google Checkout to pay by credit card.

3. Scroll down the page until the name of the game is visible. A down arrow displays to its left.

4. Click the down arrow and select **Manage Permissions** from the menu that opens (See Figure 11.20).

5. On the Google Accounts page (see Figure 11.21), click the **Revoke Access** link to the right of the game whose access you want to revoke. This page lists the permissions each game has access to. For example, the Diamond Dash game has access to Google+ Recommended People and Profile Information.

Google removes permissions for that game, which can no longer access your Google+ data. If you decide you want to play that game again, you must give Google+ permission to access your data again.

FIGURE 11.20   Select Manage Permissions from the menu.

FIGURE 11.21   Revoke access to any game you no longer wish to have access to your account data.

Summary

In this lesson, you learned how to have fun and protect your privacy playing Google+ games. Next, learn how to access Google+ on the go with Google+ Mobile.

LESSON 12

Using Google+ Mobile

In this lesson, you learn how to keep up with Google+ using your mobile phone.

Exploring Google+ Mobile

Google+ Mobile enables you to view selected Google+ data and perform selected Google+ tasks on your mobile phone. Google+ offers four free mobile options:

- ▶ Google+ Android app, for Android 2.1+ users

- ▶ Google+ iPhone app, for iPhone and iPod Touch iOS 4+ users

- ▶ Google+ Mobile web app, for Android 1.5+ users or iPhone and iPod Touch iOS3+ users

- ▶ Google+ Mobile basic web app, for Blackberry 6.0+, Nokia/Symbian, and Windows Mobile users

The mobile features available vary based on which app you use.

Although Google+ Mobile offers much of the same functionality as the web-based version of Google+, it also offers some unique features such as:

- ▶ **Huddle.** Participate in group texting, either one-on-one or with the people in one of your Google+ circles. You can invite others to a huddle or receive a notification on your status bar when someone invites you to a huddle. With Huddle, you maintain control over who can start a huddle with you: anyone on Google+, only people in your circles, or only people in your extended circles. This feature is currently available only for the Google+ Android app and Google+ iPhone app.

▶ **Instant Upload.** Upload photos and videos automatically from your phone to a private Google+ album. You can later make any photos or videos public if you choose to share them. This feature is currently available only for the Google+ Android app. See Lesson 8, "Working with Photos," for more information about Instant Upload.

▶ **Check-ins.** Check into places you visit and view posts from people who are nearby. You must give Google+ permission to share your location to use this feature. Google+ Check-ins is only available for the Android, iPhone, and iPod Touch.

For detailed instructions on how to use the specific features available for your phone, go to http://www.google.com/support/mobile and select the Google+ link.

Using the Google+ Android App

Google+ offers a mobile app for Android users that's available on Android Market at http://market.android.com/details?id=com.google.android.apps.plus. This app requires Android 2.1 and up. Figure 12.1 shows you the Google+ Android home screen.

The Google+ Android app is a full-featured application that enables you to perform a wide variety of tasks on your mobile phone. For example, you can:

▶ Participate in a huddle (group texting)

▶ Instantly upload photos to Google+

▶ View and share content on your stream (see Figure 12.2)

▶ View profiles

▶ Create and manage circles

▶ Enter and manage comments

▶ Post and delete photos

▶ View and manage notifications

FIGURE 12.1   Get mobile access to Google+ from your Android phone.

FIGURE 12.2   View and share content on your Android.

▶ Check into places (if you choose to share your location)

▶ View your nearby stream, which displays posts from people who are near you (if you choose to share your location)

Using the Google+ iPhone App

Google+ offers a mobile app for iPhone and iPod Touch users that's available on the iTunes App Store at http://itunes.apple.com/us/app/google/id447119634?ls=1&mt=8. This app requires iOS 4 and up. Figure 12.3 shows you a sample post with comments on the iPhone.

FIGURE 12.3   Post and comment on Google+ even when you're on the go.

Using the Google+ iPhone app, you can:

▶ Participate in a huddle (group texting), as shown in Figure 12.4

▶ View and share content on your stream

FIGURE 12.4   Keep the conversation going with the Google+ iPhone app.

- ▶ View profiles
- ▶ Create and manage circles
- ▶ Enter and manage comments
- ▶ Post and delete photos
- ▶ View and manage notifications
- ▶ Check into places (if you choose to share your location)
- ▶ View your nearby stream, which displays posts from people who are near you (if you choose to share your location)

Using the Google+ Mobile Web App

The Google+ Mobile web app offers limited mobile functionality for Android 1.5+ users or iPhone and iPod Touch iOS3+ users.

NOTE: **Why Are There Two Options for Android and iPhone Users?**

The mobile options available to Android, iPhone, and iPod Touch users vary based on the operating system you have. If you have a newer phone (Android 2.1+ or iPhone/iPod Touch iOS 4+), you should use the app designed for your phone rather than the Google+ Mobile web app.

To access the Google+ mobile web app, go to http://m.google.com/app/plus on your supported mobile device. Using the web app, you can do the following:

► View and share content on your stream

► View profiles

► Create and manage circles

► Enter and manage comments

► Check into places (if you choose to share your location)

► View your nearby stream, which displays posts from people who are near you (if you choose to share your location)

Using the Google+ Mobile Basic Web App

The Google+ Mobile basic web app offers limited mobile functionality for Blackberry 6.0+, Nokia/Symbian, and Windows Mobile users.

To access the basic web app, go to http://m.google.com/app/plus on your supported mobile device. Using the basic web app, you can view and share content on your stream. If you choose to share your location, you can also view your nearby stream, which displays posts from people who are near you.

Summary

In this lesson, you learned how to access Google+ from your mobile phone and download device-specific mobile apps for the Android, iPhone, and iPod Touch, as well as for Blackberry, Nokia/Symbian, and Windows Mobile users. Next, you'll explore some useful Google+ add-ons and extensions.

LESSON 13

Using Google+ Extensions and Add-Ons

In this lesson, you learn how to extend the power of Google+ with extensions, add-ons, and other useful tools.

Exploring Google+ Extensions and Add-Ons

The release of Google+ started a flurry of activity in the development community, with innovative programmers creating many useful tools that extend the functionality of Google+. For example, you can find ways to integrate Facebook and Twitter with Google+, streamline your stream, quickly reply to other users, translate posts, and much more.

CAUTION: **Google+ Extensions and Add-Ons Are Beta Versions**

Keep in mind that because Google+ is currently in beta, these tools should also be considered beta versions. If you have difficulty with a particular tool, check out its download page for updates and support information. If you're still having problems, remove the tool from your browser and try a similar tool.

NOTE: **What's the Difference Between Google+ and Google Plus?**

Be aware that some developers use the term "Google Plus" to refer to Google+. This isn't a different product; it's just another way of spelling Google+.

Exploring Google+ Chrome Extensions

If you use the Google Chrome web browser, numerous free Google+ extensions are available to make your life easier when using Google+. To install Google+ extensions for Chrome, go to the Chrome web store at https://chrome.google.com/webstore, locate the extension you want, and click the **Add to Chrome** button on the extension detail page. You must use the Chrome browser when visiting the web store to download extensions. Figure 13.1 shows a sample extension available at the web store.

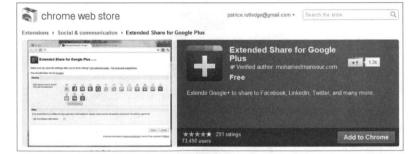

FIGURE 13.1   Chrome offers many Google+ extensions.

> NOTE: **Where Can I Download Google Chrome?**
> If you don't use Chrome, you can download it from www.google.com/chrome. This browser is available for Windows XP, Windows Vista, Windows 7, Mac OS X 10.5 or later, or Linux.

In this section, I'll introduce you to several useful Google+ Chrome extensions. To explore other extensions—including the many new extensions currently in development, visit the web store and search for "Google Plus."

Extended Share for Google Plus

Extended Share for Google Plus (https://chrome.google.com/webstore/detail/oenpjldbckebacipkfbcoppmiflglnib) enables you to quickly share your Google+ posts on other social sites such as Twitter, Facebook,

LinkedIn, Tumblr, Posterous, and more. When you install this extension, it adds a **Share On** link at the bottom of each post, as shown in Figure 13.2.

FIGURE 13.2   Share your Google+ posts on your favorite sites including Facebook and Twitter.

G+me for Google Plus

If the posts on your stream generate too many comments, you can collapse posts and comments using G+me for Google Plus (https://chrome.google.com/webstore/detail/oacdcllhgpddmlnhajiacfakhlilbicp). For example, you can click the down arrows to the left of comments (see Figure 13.3) to collapse them (see Figure 13.4).

Click to collapse

FIGURE 13.3   Click the arrow to collapse comments.

FIGURE 13.4   Comments are collapsed.

Replies and More for Google+

If you reply to posts frequently on Google+, the Replies and More for Google+ extension (https://chrome.google.com/webstore/detail/fgmhgfecnmeljhchgcjlfldjiepcfpea) makes things easier by adding a **Reply to Author** link at the end of each post, as shown in Figure 13.5.

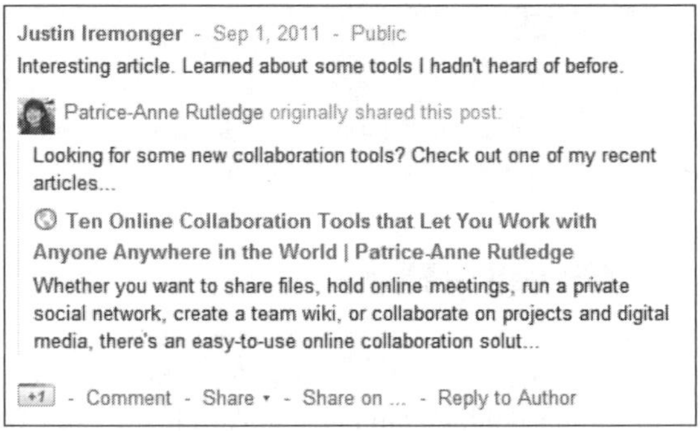

Justin Iremonger - Sep 1, 2011 - Public
Interesting article. Learned about some tools I hadn't heard of before.

Patrice-Anne Rutledge originally shared this post:

Looking for some new collaboration tools? Check out one of my recent articles...

Ten Online Collaboration Tools that Let You Work with Anyone Anywhere in the World | Patrice-Anne Rutledge
Whether you want to share files, hold online meetings, run a private social network, create a team wiki, or collaborate on projects and digital media, there's an easy-to-use online collaboration solut...

+1 - Comment - Share ▾ - Share on ... - Reply to Author

FIGURE 13.5   Quickly reply to a post author.

The "More" part of this extension adds several other useful features including a drop-down next to the **Share** link that lets you share via Twitter, Facebook, and email.

Google Plus Manager

Google Plus Manager (https://chrome.google.com/webstore/detail/mmebdhepjijdhplbheaboahdgloeoanl) extends Google+ with a variety of useful tools including keyboard shortcuts, as well as **Share**, **Reply**, and **Translate** buttons at the end of each post and a **Manage** button on the Google+ bar that enables you to quickly access numerous Google+ features. Figure 13.6 shows a sample post with these buttons.

+Photo Zoom

If you view a lot of photos on your Google+ stream, +Photo Zoom (https://chrome.google.com/webstore/detail/njoglkofocgopmdfjnbifnicbickbola) lets you view enlarged photo pop-ups any time you pause your mouse over a photo, as shown in Figure 13.7.

New buttons to share, reply, and translate

FIGURE 13.6   Share, reply, or translate at the click of a button.

FIGURE 13.7   Enlarge photos from the stream on the fly.

Exploring Google+ Add-Ons for Mozilla Firefox

Although Google Chrome offers the widest variety of extensions for Google+, Mozilla Firefox users have several options as well.

To install Google+ add-ons for Firefox, go to the **Firefox Add-Ons** page at https://addons.mozilla.org, locate the add-on you want, and click the

Add to Firefox button on the add-on detail page. You must use the Firefox browser to download these add-ons. Figure 13.8 shows a sample add-on detail page.

FIGURE 13.8   Firefox also offers several Google+ add-ons.

Some interesting Firefox add-ins to check out:

▸ **Start Google Plus** (https://addons.mozilla.org/en-US/firefox/ addon/start-google-plus). Integrate Google+ with Facebook and Twitter and find Facebook friends who are on Google+.

▸ **gplusmute** (https://addons.mozilla.org/en-US/firefox/addon/ gplusmute). Mute messages in your Google+ stream.

▸ **G++** (http://gplusplus.me/download.html). Integrate Google+ with Facebook and Twitter (see Figure 13.9).

![Stream interface with Google+, facebook, twitter checkboxes and Refresh Stream button; text "Post to your Facebook & Twitter account along with any Google Plus circle(s) with G++ !!!!"; Click to Post to FB/Twitter; Acquaintances + Add more people; Share button.]

FIGURE 13.9   Integrate Google+ with Facebook and Twitter.

Exploring Other Google+ Tools

If you're looking for more ways to enhance your Google+ experience, here's a quick roundup of other tools worth investigating:

▶ **gplus.to** (http://gplus.to). Create an easy to remember URL for Google+, such as http://gplus.to/PatriceRutledge.

▶ **Google Plus Widget** (http://widgetsplus.com). Add a Google+ widget to your website or blog, encouraging people to connect with you on Google+ (see Figure 13.10).

FIGURE 13.10   Let your site visitors know about your Google+ profile.

▶ **Plusya** (http://plusya.com). Create a shortened Google+ URL with analytics, which allow you to monitor your traffic and see how many visitors you have had.

▶ **Find your+** (http://findyourplus.com). Search for other Google+ users by country, city, occupation, and more (see Figure 13.11).

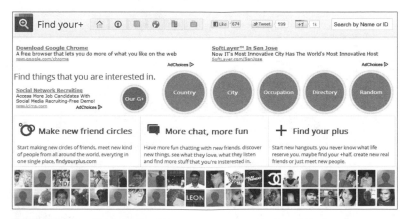

FIGURE 13.11   Find new and future friends on this Google+ people directory.

Summary

In this lesson, you learned how to extend the functionality of Google+ with extensions, add-ons, and other tools.

Index

sending game invitations and
requests, 204

sharing game activity on
Games stream, 207-210

Games stream, sharing game
activity, 207-210

Google Accounts page, 57

Google Chrome, downloading, 224

Google Plus Manager, 226

Google Plus Widget, 229

Google Privacy, managing privacy
settings, 68-69

Google+, 3-5

allowing to search for
connected accounts, 79

signing into, 13-14

signing out of, 132

Google+ Android app, 216-218

Google+ bar, 5, 123-124

accessing features, 128-129

feedback, 130

help, 130

sharing content, 129

viewing notifications, 124-128

Google+ Chrome extensions, 224

Google+ circles, 33-34

adding people to, 36-38

email contacts, 40-45

*from Google+ profiles,
49-51*

Incoming stream, 47

notifications menu, 45-47

suggestions, 39

creating, 34-36

deleting, 54-55

editing name and description,
53-54

sending invitations to
friends, 49

viewing people who added
you to their circles, 51

viewing people in your
circles, 51

Google+ iPhone app, 218-220

Google+ Mobile, 215

check-ins, 216

huddle, 215

Instant Upload, 216

Google+ Mobile basic web
app, 220

Google+ profile button, adding to
websites, 30-31

Google+ profiles, 15-17

adding links to, 22-25

adding people to Google+
circles, 49-51

editing, 17

About tab, 17-20

managing privacy settings, 66

privacy, 22

Y-Z

Sams**Teach Yourself**

from Sams Publishing

Sams **Teach Yourself in 10 Minutes** offers straightforward, practical answers for fast results.

These small books of 250 pages or less offer tips that point out shortcuts and solutions, cautions that help you avoid common pitfalls, and notes that explain additional concepts and provide additional information. By working through the 10-minute lessons, you learn everything you need to know quickly and easily!

When you only have time for the answers, Sams Teach Yourself books are your best solution.

Visit **informit.com/samsteachyourself** for a complete listing of the products available.

FREE Online Edition

Your purchase of *Sams Teach Yourself Google+ in 10 Minutes* includes access to a free online edition for 45 days through the Safari Books Online subscription service. Nearly every Sams book is available online through Safari Books Online, along with more than 5,000 other technical books and videos from publishers such as Addison-Wesley Professional, Cisco Press, Exam Cram, IBM Press, O'Reilly, Prentice Hall, and Que.

SAFARI BOOKS ONLINE allows you to search for a specific answer, cut and paste code, download chapters, and stay current with emerging technologies.

Activate your FREE Online Edition at www.informit.com/safarifree

> **STEP 1:** Enter the coupon code: HFOQYYG.

> **STEP 2:** New Safari users, complete the brief registration form. Safari subscribers, just log in.

If you have difficulty registering on Safari or accessing the online edition, please e-mail customer-service@safaribooksonline.com